D1600470

Pastoral Care for Survivors of a Traumatic Death

Pastoral Care for Survivors of a Traumatic Death

A Challenge for Contemporary Pastors

JEONGHYUN PARK

WIPF *&* STOCK · Eugene, Oregon

BV
4330
.P37
2017

PASTORAL CARE FOR SURVIVORS OF A TRAUMATIC DEATH
A Challenge for Contemporary Pastors

Copyright © 2017 Jeonghyun Park. All rights reserved. Except for brief
quotations in critical publications or reviews, no part of this book may
be reproduced in any manner without prior written permission from the
publisher. Write: Permissions, Wipf and Stock Publishers, 199 W. 8th Ave.,
Suite 3, Eugene, OR 97401.

Wipf & Stock
An Imprint of Wipf and Stock Publishers
199 W. 8th Ave., Suite 3
Eugene, OR 97401

www.wipfandstock.com

PAPERBACK ISBN: 978-1-5326-3016-3
HARDCOVER ISBN: 978-1-5326-3018-7
EBOOK ISBN: 978-1-5326-3017-0

Manufactured in the U.S.A.   NOVEMBER 6, 2017

[Scripture quotations are from] New Revised Standard Version Bible,
copyright © 1989 National Council of the Churches of Christ in the United
States of America. Used by permission. All rights reserved worldwide.

Contents

Acknowledgments

This book is the result of my pastoral desires and struggles while wrestling with pastoral challenges that I faced when providing pastoral care for congregants who had lost loved ones to suicide or various forms of unexpected traumatic death. The pastoral ministry at Fair Oaks United Methodist Church in California is one of the great blessings in my life, especially the opportunity it gives me to share God's comfort and hope with those who are mourning and grieving the loss of their loved ones as their spiritual servant. I am deeply grateful to the members of Fair Oaks United Methodist Church for their whole-hearted support that enabled me to complete this writing project. Without their deep care and strong support, I would not have undertaken this study. I am indebted to numerous members of the congregation who have read my manuscript repeatedly. I especially would like to thank to Nancy Edward for her warm heart and wonderful assistance; Judy Shearer for always being willing to help me go over the draft; and Gretchen Hatfield, chair of the Staff Parish Relations Committee, along with the other members of this committee. They all understood the importance of this study and encouraged me to finish this journey.

I am also indebted to the Council of Clergy Development for the California Nevada Annual Conference of the United Methodist Church. They have generously supported my doctoral studies by granting me a scholarship. The General Board of Higher Education and Ministry, which supports scholarship within the United Methodist Church, has provided great additional support to my studies. I hope that this book will be a small token of my gratitude for the great blessing that I have received from the California Nevada Annual Conference and the United Methodist Church. In particular, I would like to express my sincere appreciation to Rev. Tina Ballagh, Rev. Kelly Love, and several of my circuit colleagues who were willing to share stories from their ministries related to traumatic death and other case studies.

I couldn't imagine finishing this writing project without the support of Dr. Scott Sullender, my academic advisor. His vast scholarship and his specialty in grief counseling greatly helped me find my academic interest in the issue of traumatic death, and he guided me on this long journey. Dr. Andrew Sung Park inspired me with his humility and his extensive knowledge of research on pastoral (spiritual) care. I am also thankful to Dr. Kirsten Oh and Dr. Daniel Schipani for their pastoral insights and encouragement. And, I am grateful to Kathy McKay for her professional copyediting work on this book.

Many colleagues have expressed their support and reminded me of the importance of pastoral care for survivors of a traumatic death. I want to thank all my colleagues and my ministry partners in various pastoral care ministries. I especially give thanks to my local church's Caring Ministry team leaders—Mary McCollum, Betty Phillips, Loretta Dodge, and Rachele Dotty (Life Challenge ministry leaders)—for their compassionate, caring ministry for those who are in great need of spiritual care and support. I hope that this small book will be an additional pastoral and spiritual resource book for their great ministry.

Finally, I give thanks to my family. My mother and father are my Christian faith heroes and the spiritual pillars of my spiritual life. They are the root of my pastoral journey and my calling to pastoral ministry. I am also very thankful to my brothers and my sisters-in-law for their ongoing prayers and hands-on assistance.

My wife, Yougjae Kim, blesses me constantly with her love, care, and spiritual wisdom. I couldn't have begun this project without her deep understanding and support of this pastoral matter. I am blessed to be her husband, friend, and life-long partner. I am also thankful to my two sons, Jacob and Joshua, for their patience and for understanding when I couldn't spend more time playing with them at the playground while I was working on this project. Now I will be able to spend more time playing with my boys.

Whether we define death as our enemy or as something else, we have to accept its reality and redefine ourselves after we have encountered it. As we mature, we inevitably experience that we are not who we once were. In the same way, the power of death requires us to adapt ourselves to our new reality and to have a new understanding of ourselves after a loss. But, the most important thing to remember is that God never changes. As Christians, we believe that God is always with us, no matter what challenges we go through. When we grieve over the loss of a loved one, our God listens to our cries and also cries with us. This is what I believe and what I have learned from this project, and I confidently claim what Immanuel God means to us in our life and faith journey.

Jeong Park

Introduction

This book focuses on *traumatic death*. I argue that sudden, traumatic death requires a different type of grief and spiritual care than ordinary death and bereavement. "Ordinary" death, which is more often an expected loss, usually occurs in the context of the developmental stages of life. The grief associated with traumatic death, however, has unique characteristics because this type of death is an unnatural, unanticipated, and violent event. Examples of traumatic death include topics that are difficult to discuss, such as suicide. In this book, I focus on suicide as illustrative of the dynamics of sudden traumatic death.

In most cases, an unnatural and traumatic death has a huge emotional and psychological impact on the family and other people closely connected to the deceased. A violent sudden death is typically experienced as a deep wound by the survivors or even as a "transgression"—as someone stepping across the personal boundary of safety. A sudden violent death is more likely to provoke the spiritually despairing question in survivors, Why? Predictable death and normal grief counseling situations are not the focus of this book. Nor are the dying and death situations caused by chronic illness, aging, long-term disabilities, or medical conditions. The narrow scope of this is designed to provide better guidance for the Christian pastor faced with offering pastoral care in the situation of a traumatic death. This project is focused on parish ministers, particularly clergy in the United Methodist Church. Although not developed for an interfaith context, this model may be applicable to interfaith contexts such as general hospital chaplaincy.

Pastors are called to care for souls. The traditional term for this is *cura animarum*. In Christian spirituality, death is recognized as a part of life. However, death is never an easy situation in the ministry of pastoral care, not for the Christian believer who is seeking help nor for the pastor. I believe that the best and the most important pastoral care skill to have in dealing with life-and-death situations is pastoral presence. The great Jewish philosopher and theologian Martin Buber, who strongly emphasized the "I and Thou relationship" in spiritual care ministry, had the following experience, as described by Maurice Friedman:

> Just before World War I, a young man came to see Buber after Buber had had a morning of mystic ecstasy. Buber was friendly and attentive; he answered the questions the young man put. But he failed to guess the question the young man did not put. After such a morning of mystic ecstasy, which was customary for him in those days, he was not really present in spirit. Later, he learned this was a question of life and death—not that the young man had committed suicide, as some imagine. He was killed at the front, as Buber told me himself, out of despair that did not oppose its own death.
>
> Buber took this as a judgment not just of that moment but of the whole way of living that splits the exalted hours from the everyday hours. "What after all does a person who is in despair but comes to see one hope for but a presence which says in spite of all there is meaning," he asked. Not reality, not philosophy, not wise words, but a presence. That was the judgment on a way of life in which he was not fully present.[1]

---

1. Friedman, *Martin Buber and the Human Sciences*, 7–8.

Ambiguous Death

A sudden traumatic death creates a profound and complicated spiritual situation for surviving family members. The family and friends of the deceased person face a psychological, emotional, and spiritual crisis; they need to accept the painful reality and then to find meaning in the midst of the chaos and confusion. The loved ones of a person who died suddenly and traumatically need the care and support of their church. Yet, for the congregants and their pastors, sudden violent death, particularly suicide, is confusing. Sudden deaths are often treated as situations requiring crisis counseling. In many cases, sudden tragic deaths are not fully embraced and accepted by the church. Suicide can be a controversial theological issue. Thus, in some churches certain forms of traumatic death, particularly suicide, are still viewed as taboo and as an immoral and sinful act.

A Korean United Methodist Church pastor shared with me his experience of officiating at a memorial service for a man who had committed suicide. The deceased and his family had been going to a Korean Presbyterian church, but their home church minister refused to hold a service for the deceased and his family. Their minister's reason was simple—suicide is a sinful act against God. The family couldn't find any pastor or church willing to hold a funeral or memorial service in their own town. Finally, the family was able to meet with my Methodist pastor friend in a nearby town, and he officiated at an appropriate service that allowed them to say goodbye to their loved one. This episode illustrates how problematic sudden death can be, particularly in conservative ethnic Christian communities.

As another example of how the church views suicide, the Catholic Church believes that suicide contradicts the natural inclination of the human being to live. It is contrary not only to the just love of self but also to the love of the living God. The Catechism of the Catholic Church describes its official theological stance on suicide as follows:

Everyone is responsible for his life before God who has given it to him. We are stewards, not owners, of the life God has entrusted to us. It is not ours to dispose of. Suicide offends love of neighbors because it unjustly breaks the ties of solidarity with family, nation, and other human societies to which we continue to have obligations. If suicide is committed with the intention of setting an example, especially to the young, it also takes on the gravity of scandal. Voluntary co-operation in suicide is contrary to the moral law. Grave psychological disturbances, anguish, or grave fear of hardship, suffering, or torture can diminish the responsibility of the one committing suicide. We should not despair of the eternal salvation of persons who have taken their own lives. By ways known to Him alone, God can provide the opportunity for salutary repentance. The Church prays for persons who have taken their own lives.[2]

The challenging reality is that today there is more sudden violent death than ever before. Here are some statistics about sudden death in the United States:

- According to the Centers for Disease Control and Prevention (CDC), nearly 4,000 U.S. infants die suddenly and unexpectedly each year. We often refer to these deaths as sudden unexpected infant death (SUID). Although the causes of death in many of these children can't be explained, most occur while the infant is sleeping in an unsafe sleeping environment.[3]

- In 2013 . . . 41,149 suicides were reported, making suicide the 10th leading cause of death for Americans. . . . [From 2000 to 2012,] the rate generally increased and by 2013 stood at 12.6 deaths per 100,000.[4]

- In 2013, the United States Department of Veterans Affairs released a study that covered suicides from 1999 to 2010 that

2. Roman Catholic Church, *Cathechism of the Catholic Church*, para. 2280–83.

3. Centers for Disease Control and Prevention, "About SUID and SIDS."

4. American Foundation for Suicide Prevention, "Facts and Figures."

stated that roughly 22 veterans were committing suicide per day, or one every 65 minutes. A recent analysis found a suicide rate among veterans of about 30 per 100,000 people per year, compared with the civilian rate of 14 per 100,000.[5]

- The U.S. homicide rate, which has declined substantially since 1992 from a rate per 100,000 persons of 9.8 to 4.8 in 2010, is still among the highest in the industrialized world. There were 13,716 homicides in the United States in 2013.[6]

PASTORS ARE ILL PREPARED

As a result of the growth in incidents of violent death, the number of people experiencing complicated grief is also growing. Pastors are expected to handle many different kinds of pastoral care situations. Caring for the bereaved is at the heart of pastoral ministry. Although most pastors are trained to handle grief, few are trained to handle sudden death and complicated grief. Yet, this is the reality that pastors find themselves in more and more, and not just in hospitals or as military chaplains but also in their local church ministries. For example, I experienced five unexpected and sudden deaths in my congregation in 2014. One person was diagnosed with cancer of the pancreas and given just a month to live; she was only fifty years old when she died. Three young men committed suicide that same year. A fifth person died of a brain aneurysm. These sudden, tragic, and painful events are the realities that made me decide to address traumatic death in my dissertation/project for my Doctor of Ministry degree through San Francisco Theological Seminary. In particular, the suicides of the three young men shocked their family members but were also emotionally devastating to the entire congregation. These deaths rocked our faith in God! This challenging situation is not unique to my personal ministry. Most pastors have to deal with similar challenges.

5. Wikipedia, "United States Military Veteran Suicide."
6. Wikipedia, "Crime in the United States."

I have come to realize that most pastors have never had training in suicide grief support. I certainly had not. I have also learned that although most pastors are trained in general grief theory, they are not trained to counsel people experiencing "traumatic grief." These painful events bring the loved ones face to face with death and the necessity of finding hope and God's mercy and grace in the midst of chaos, questions, and confusion.

As another example, a research project on sudden bereavement was conducted by University of British Columbia professor Darrin Leheman and associates. The researchers interviewed forty people who had lost a spouse and fifty-four people who had lost a child in a car accident four to seven years earlier. The purpose of the interviews was to gather information concerning the support that the survivors had received. The results of the interviews revealed an important lesson. The study reported that 62 percent of the bereaved individuals reported that some of the "support" was not helpful to them. This included others giving them advice, blithely encouraging their recovery from the loss, and even making rude remarks.[7] This study reflects the reality that most people—including pastors—are not well trained in how to provide appropriate support to those suffering from sudden bereavement. I believe that the importance of providing good pastoral care and spiritual presence in cases of sudden death is an issue related to improving a pastor's competency but also an important concern for the life and growth of the church in general. If pastors do not know how to be fully present with those who are angry and despairing, those who are struggling to sense the presence of God, this may result in people losing faith. Based on my parish ministry experience, I would say that effective pastoral care ministry is a more powerful message than well-crafted Sunday sermons.

In this book, which is a revised version of my dissertation/project, I explore the pastoral challenges raised by the grief associated with the traumatic death of a loved one. I present specific, relevant examples of pastoral care and counseling that pastors can use as models when supporting those who have lost a loved one to

7. Lehman et al., "Social Support for the Bereaved," 438–46.

a traumatic death such as suicide. Moreover, I offer new insights and practical pastoral care models for families needing recovery and healing, as well as meaningful rituals to help families and friends grieving the traumatic death of a loved one. Responding to traumatic death is a powerful opportunity for pastors and survivors to explore God's grace and mercy in the moment.

Outline of This Book

Chapter 1 deals with traumatic death in context. I define how I understand traumatic death and explore the reality of traumatic death in the United States. Diverse cultural understandings and approaches to the issue of traumatic death are introduced. The growing cultural diversity of this nation and the church has led scholars to view the grief process as more idiosyncratic than universal. I also review in this chapter the impact of unresolved loss on those left behind.

Chapter 2 mostly focuses on psychological perspectives on grief connected with traumatic death. This chapter explores the research and clinical literature on the nature of loss, grief, and bereavement. Grief studies have evolved in recent years as a result of the growing incidence of traumatic death. So, I survey the current literature and in particular focus on how grief and bereavement are different in the context of traumatic death compared to ordinary death. I explain the nature of complicated grief, which is more likely to develop in the case of traumatic death.

Chapter 3 explores the challenges of traumatic death from the viewpoint of theology. Traumatic death, more than ordinary death, prompts questions in survivors around theodicy, such as, How can a good God cause or allow such evil? Other questions that might surface in a traumatic death situation are: Where is God in this tragic death? Why did God let my son take his own life? Why is this suffering happening to us? Where is God in our agony? If we have to admit the reality of what happened, where can we find God's grace, mercy, power, and justice in this tragedy? These are some of the questions that people ask when they face traumatic loss. Suicides and deaths by sudden violence focus these issues sharply. I believe that the loved ones of the victims of traumatic death can be comforted if they receive help with their questions concerning a "helpless God" and a "cruel God." Loved ones often seek such answers from their pastor. The job of pastors is not just to provide care but also to help people find spiritual answers that are meaningful, genuine, and sensitive. Furthermore, pastors are challenged to help survivors find God's compassionate grace and mercy in the midst of their suffering.

Chapter 4 introduces the project I designed and conducted, which was a six-week traumatic grief counseling course for pastors. This course provides principles and guidelines for offering spiritual support to parishioners and community members who are dealing with traumatic loss and grief and identifies the spiritual, psychological, emotional, and cultural challenges pastors and other spiritual caregivers face in providing this type of pastoral care. I tested this curriculum with a group of United Methodist Church clergypersons in California. Chapter 4 includes the curriculum and excerpts from the group discussions. The curriculum consisted of six one-hour sessions. In each session, I offered an introduction to the week's topic and one participant presented a case for discussion. Some of the case discussions were followed by reflections and evaluative comments. These were the six sessions:

- Week 1: Traumatic death vs. natural death
- Week 2: Characteristics and patterns of traumatic death
- Week 3: Pastoral responses to concerns about human evil and the desire for revenge
- Week 4: Ministering to those who have lost loved ones to suicide
- Week 5: Pastoral care and counseling for families after a traumatic loss
- Week 6: Helpful rituals for families

In the final chapter, I integrate my practical experience from the project with the background information provided in the earlier chapters concerning cultural, psychological, and pastoral theology. I reflect on where to go from here and on how the curriculum I developed on pastoral care in cases of traumatic death for the use of pastors, pastoral counselors, and spiritual caregivers might be helpful to pastors and congregation members offering spiritual care to those who have lost a loved one to a traumatic death.

CONCLUSION

Traumatic death is a sudden and horrific event that brings loved ones face to face with a dreadful death and leaves them with a desperate yearning to find hope and grace in the midst of the tragedy, disbelief, chaos, and confusion. Pastors and spiritual caregivers are called to be "bridges" to connect God with the human reality through their *spiritual presence*. It is imperative that pastors prepare themselves for this extremely difficult task that is unfortunately becoming more needed in our nation, touching the lives of our congregations and our communities everywhere. If pastors do not know how to be fully present with those who are in anger and despair, those who are struggling to sense God's presence or are furious with God, this inability to serve others well may have profound consequences, including the loss of faith among people grieving a traumatic death. My ultimate goal is that this book will serve as a resource for Christian pastors that answers this daunting question: *How can pastors be spiritually present when they encounter situations of horrific and traumatic death, situations that are accompanied by complex grief issues?* It is my hope that this book will blaze the trail in providing helpful, appropriate, and much-needed tools for pastors so they can enhance their understanding of traumatic grief and embrace the unspoken need for *spiritual presence* in the context of traumatic deaths. I invite you to join me on this journey.

1

Traumatic Death in the Larger Social and Cultural Context

This chapter places traumatic death in its larger cultural and social context. I provide definitions and interpretations and suggest terms that best describe the characteristics of traumatic death. It is important for pastors to develop their own interpretation of traumatic death so they can promptly offer their unique form of care to those in need, helping shepherd the surviving loved ones through horrific and unexpected times.

This chapter then explores the reality of traumatic death, focusing on violence in the United States. Various cultural and sociological understandings are introduced. The growing cultural diversity of this nation and of the church has led most scholars to view grief as more idiosyncratic than universal. The spiritually disruptive impact of unresolved loss due to traumatic death is also reviewed in this chapter, using as a case example an actual and rather well-known case of death by suicide.

DEFINITION OF TRAUMATIC DEATH

Psychological trauma is an affliction of the powerless. At the moment of trauma, the victim is rendered helpless by overwhelming force. When the force is that of nature, we call it a natural disaster. When the force is that of other human beings, we speak of atrocity.[1] According to the *Diagnostic and Statistical Manual of Mental Disorders* (*DSM*-5), trauma is defined as exposure to actual or threatened death, serious injury, or sexual violence in one (or more) of the following ways:

1. Directly experiencing the traumatic event(s),

2. Witnessing in person the event(s) as it occurred to others;

3. Learning about a traumatic event(s) to a close family member or a close friend—in the case of an actual or threatened death of a family member or friend, the event(s) must have been violent or accidental;

4. Experiencing repeated or extreme exposure to aversive details of the traumatic event(s).[2]

Trauma inevitably brings loss, and those who lose important people in their lives face a new void in their relationships with friends, family, and/or community. Traumatic losses rupture the ordinary sequence of generations and defy the ordinary social conventions of bereavement. A traumatic loss is one that is sudden, unanticipated, violent, and outside the normal range of experience. These losses profoundly overwhelm the resources of the bereaved, leaving them feeling helpless.[3] Scott Sullender defines traumatic death as characterized by five signs:

1. Trauma is unexpected. It is about change, compressed change, too much change in too short a time.

2. Trauma comes with an element of horror; it is repulsive to our basic human sense of goodness, in this sense very out of the ordinary—violence and death.

---

1. Herman, *Trauma and Recovery*, 32.

2. American Psychiatric Association, *Diagnostic and Statistical Manual*, 272.

3. Gilbert, "Traumatic Loss and the Family." For more information on the concept of differential grief, see Gilbert's article on grief within families, "'We've Had the Same Loss.'"

3. Traumatic death provokes an intense, fearful reaction.

4. Trauma brings a sense of helplessness or powerlessness.

5. Trauma leads people to be overwhelmed, at least temporarily.[4]

Trauma makes one feel unable to cope, and it may create a freeze reaction usually seen in animals; at other times, it can lead to a paralysis that may go on for weeks. Trauma definitely can cause survivors to feel immobilized and unable to make decisions.

Psychiatrist Edward K. Rynearson defines traumatic death as violent dying, and this form of dying has three characteristics that begin with V:

1. violence: The act of dying is injurious,

2. violation: The act of dying is transgressive.

3. volition: The act of dying is willful (suicide or homicide) or the result of irresponsible negligence (most fatal accidents are due to human error.)[5]

According to Rynearson, the reaction to a traumatic death is understood as the result of a violent act. For example, suicide is one of the most agonizing kinds of death for surviving spouses, parents, and other family members, and it can result in shame, anger, and guilt. It is an example of a disenfranchised or publicly unacknowledged loss, thus making it harder for the survivors to mourn. In funerals or memorial services, many times the true reason for a death (suicide) is hidden from public view. The social stigma, trauma distress, and avoidance of public acknowledgment of the cause of death can last for many years.[6]

In this book, I narrow down the scope of what I consider traumatic death by focusing primarily on violent acts that are either caused by an external force or are the result of an internal willful choice (as in suicide). As a result of this kind of traumatic death,

4. Sullender, "Loss, Grief and Trauma."

5. Rynearson, *Retelling Violent Death*, 21.

6. Ibid., 119.

loved ones are severely traumatized psychologically, emotionally, and spiritually by the impact and force of the violent death.

The survivors of a traumatic death have to deal with a number of complex issues and problems, unlike those who survive an expected death, because the grief process resulting from a traumatic death is very different from that resulting from a natural, anticipated death. According to Albert Y. Hsu, a traumatic and sudden death creates special problems for the survivors that complicate the grief process. He writes:

> The grief response following sudden and traumatic death is often intense simply because there is little or no opportunity to prepare for the loss, say good-bye, finish unfinished business, or prepare for bereavement. Families and friends are suddenly forced to face the loss of a loved one instantaneously and without warning. This type of loss can generate intense initial grief responses such as shock, denial, numbness, anger, and an explosion of emotions. Traumatic grief is not a linear process, a straight path mapped out from one starting point to a final destination. Rather, it is a journey filled with twists and turns, unexpected detours and dead ends that force us back over ground we thought we had already covered. Often several different, overlapping emotions may assault us at once, and we find ourselves caught in cycles of good days and bad.[7]

As the bereavement process unfolds, the bereaved person may suffer from "survivor guilt," wondering why they survived when others have died and believing that they could have or should have done more to prevent the tragedy.[8] Although traumatic death has always been a part of death and has always involved a grief process, traumatic death and loss require a different type of grief and spiritual care than ordinary death and bereavement. Later in this chapter, I will focus on a case study of suicide as an illustration of the dynamics of traumatic death.

7. Hsu, *Grieving Suicide*, 27.
8. Dyer, "Dealing with Sudden, Accidental or Traumatic Death."

Storytelling plays a major role in bereavement. It is how mourners process their sorrow and make memories. Yet, storytelling is dramatically different in situations of natural dying and traumatic death. It is necessary for pastors to understand this difference so they can effectively guide those in grief. In the case of a natural death, the re-enactment story contains a complex plot that allows many participants to fashion a story together. They gather around the dying family members to prevent or prepare for death. When death finally comes naturally, ideally each family member has had an opportunity to engage in a final role as comforter and protector so that the person dying will not die alone.

The narrative structure of traumatic dying, in contrast, puts the spotlight on the death itself. According to Rynearson, unlike natural dying, the story of traumatic dying is itself the main focus in the early stages of bereavement. When a death is violent, the survivors have to deal with feelings of terror.[9] With violent dying, the deceased and the family are isolated from one another by a rush of action that does not allow a collective attempt to prevent or prepare for death. There is no opportunity to gather and create a dying story together or even to be there as the family member is dying.[10] Violent dying is not only a tragic and unwanted ending to the life story of the deceased but is carried forward as a chaotic and unacceptable ending of vitality and identity in the life stories of the survivors.

Glennys Howarth discusses some of the immediate issues that arise in a situation of sudden, traumatic death:

> In the context of sudden death, survivors often need the information produced by the coroner's inquest in order to make sense of their own future. That is, they need to know how, when and where the deceased died. What the inquest may not provide, however, and what is often central to a bereaved person's sense of biographical continuity, is the knowledge of 'why' their loved one died. If . . . the key characteristic of the coroner's role

9. Rynearson, "Accommodation to Unnatural Death."
10. Rynearson, *Retelling Violent Death*, 20–21.

is to distinguish between natural and unnatural death, this does not entail an understanding of why the person died, nor does it apportion blame—a future area of tension between legal requirements and expectations of the bereaved.[11]

Many unanswered questions starting with the word *why* overwhelm the survivors of a person who died a traumatic death as they desperately attempt to make sense of their loved one's death. They often ask questions such as, Why did it happen? Why my loved one? How did it happen? What can I do to prevent this from happening again? A traumatic death is also more likely to provoke spiritually despairing questions, such as, Why did God allow this horror to happen to us? In chapter 3, I provide a compilation of tools and stories to help bridge the huge spiritual gap that can be created between survivors of traumatic death and their ability to retain or heal their relationship with God. Pastors can facilitate through shared experience the exploration of God's grace and mercy in the midst of such horrific circumstances.

SUICIDE IN THE UNITED STATES

I have defined traumatic death as a consequence of crises initiated by acts of violence caused either by an external force or by an internal willful choice, as in suicide. We live in a violent society where violent crimes, homicides, suicides, and domestic violence occur around the clock. Such events may affect us at any time and change our lives forever. In fact, no one is free from the potential danger of traumatic loss. Pastors and faith community leaders are generally aware of this reality in their parish ministries. Here, I review the reality of one form of violence in the United States—suicide. How big a problem is it? Much research has been conducted on suicide in U.S. society, especially in the contexts of race, economics, and social environment.

---

11. Howarth, *Death and Dying*, 170–71.

Death by suicide is the tenth leading cause of death in the United States. The rate of suicide declined between 1900 and 2000, but since 2000 there has been, for the most part, a steady increase. To date, there is no way to count and report unsuccessful attempts at suicide. The Centers for Disease Control requests information from hospitals every year on numbers of "non-fatal injuries resulting from self-harm behavior," and the American Foundation for Suicide Prevention estimates that approximately one million people in the United States intentionally hurt themselves each year.[12] Middle-aged White males represent the largest number of completed suicides. Note that suicide ranks as the tenth cause of death in the United States, and, sadly, it ranks second for young people. An average of one person every 12.8 minutes killed themselves in the United States in the year 2013.[13]

HOW DO EXPERIENCES OF DYING, DEATH, AND GRIEF DIFFER?

Every society and community has its own cultural understandings that help it interpret traumatic grief, loss, and death. Sociologist Glennys Howarth raises important questions in her book *Death and Dying: A Sociological Introduction,* such as, How do experiences of dying, death and grief differ in different societies? What accounts for these differences? How is death, in its various dimensions, managed within societies?[14] From a cultural perspective, another appropriate question would be: How do experiences of traumatic death, loss, and grief differ in different cultures?

Death is common to all persons, and the dying process elicits grief and mourning in every culture. The individual's way of dying is as unique as are human personalities. David Augsburger, in his book *Pastoral Counseling across Cultures,* points out that in every culture, the introverted are less likely to express fears and

---

12. American Foundation for Suicide Prevention, "Facts and Figures."

13. American Association of Suicidology, "U.S.A. Suicide: 2013 Official Final Data."

14. Howarth, *Death and Dying,* 2–3.

grief; extroverts are more likely to question, protest, converse, and commune with others in their grief work. Variations in hostility, negativism, and irritability, for example, occur in every culture and become more distinct and pronounced in the dying experience.[15] For example, Augsburger discusses differences between cultural attitudes in Japan and the United States toward the classic "stages of dying" process. He writes:

> Americans prefer open confrontation, even with tragic news. Americans can't stand ambiguity, while Japanese are used to it. Westerners recognize and express open anger, while Japanese prefer subtle negotiation or cautious irritability [confrontation]. Where Westerners, whether theists or agnostics, still bargain with God, the Japanese do not. Their cosmology does not offer a sovereign power who can be swayed by human strategies of persuasion, so they move from hope and suspicion directly to depression. . . . Americans believe that they have the right to know everything that affects them and their destiny.[16]

Culture influences not only how people interpret the meaning of a traumatic event but also how individuals and communities express their reactions to trauma. According to Kris Sieckert, although reactions to trauma seem to be common to all cultures and are based in the physiology of human beings, manifestations of these responses may differ significantly. Sieckert writes:

> Culture forms a context through which the traumatized individuals or communities view and judge their own response. If people think that the society around them will not accept them as victims, there is a tendency to withdraw and be silent. Culture may affect the responses of those who identify themselves as "non-traumatized" as well as of the traumatized. This is a critical issue for many people who are victims. Their own culture or the culture in which they live may reject or stigmatize them, which may be perceived as an additional injury. Cultures may help define healthy pathways to new lives

15. Augsburger, *Pastoral Counseling across Cultures*, 66–67.
16. Ibid.

after trauma. Cultural routines and traditions may aid survivors of a tragedy in feeling re-oriented or rendering life predictable.[17]

People's reactions to a traumatic experience may be shaped by their cultural perspective. Specifically, culture

a. Influences what type of threat is perceived as traumatic
b. Influences how individuals and communities interpret the meaning of a traumatic event and how they express their reactions to the event
c. Forms a context through which traumatized individuals or communities view and judge their own response
d. May help define healthy pathways to new lives after trauma[18]

Lisa Athan, a grief recovery specialist and founder of Grief Speaks, argues that each culture has its own traditions, rituals, and ways of expressing grief and mourning.[19] For example, African Americans may believe in the concept of the "living dead"—people who help those who have recently died move to the next world. Many Hispanic survivors commemorate the loss of a loved one with promises or commitments. These promises are taken very seriously, and those who fail to honor them are considered sinners. In the European American tradition, people tend to wear dark clothing during memorial services, although this trend has shifted in recent years to colorful clothing that helps create an atmosphere of celebration and hope.[20] Among Asian Americans, common practices include showing respect for the body by dressing the deceased in warm clothes and using a watertight casket. Athan reports that "stoic attitudes are common, and depression may result from the internalization of grief."[21] Family and friends gather together to show respect for the spirit, share their memories and love of the

17. Sieckert, "Cultural Perspectives on Trauma and Crisis Response."
18. Grief Speaks, "Understanding Cultural Issues in Death."
19. Ibid.
20. Grief Speaks, "Cultures and Grief."
21. Grief Speaks, "Understanding Cultural Issues in Death."

deceased, and give thanks to those who were present at the memorial or funeral service.

Since suicide is one of the most tragic types of traumatic death, I review here the sociological literature on suicide in the United States. Durkheim was the first sociologist to investigate the social factors of suicide. He argued that suicide is not simply the result of individual psychological distress or a disordered personality but is a consequence of social disorder.[22] In his book *The Rules of Sociological Method*, Durkheim argues:

> [Social facts] are indeed not inaccurately represented by rates of births, marriages and suicides, that is, by the result obtained after dividing the average annual total of marriages, births, and voluntary homicides by the number of persons of an age to marry, produce children, or commit suicide. Since each one of these statistics includes without distinction all individual cases, the individual circumstances which may have played some part in producing the phenomenon cancel each other out and consequently do not contribute to determining the nature of the phenomenon. What it expresses is a certain state of the collective mind.[23]

Durkheim believes that marriage and suicide are clearly social facts even though they appear to be purely individual and private matters. Statistics enable us to view suicide as a social phenomenon. Durkheim found a correlation between high suicide rates and other factors in society, such as marriage and divorce rates, single status, urban living, and social and religious integration. He showed, for example, that suicide rates are higher in countries with weaker religious and social integration and are also higher among single people than married people. His research goal was to explain how society coerces the individual and how the level of social integration in a particular society influences the extent of suicide.[24]

22. Howarth, *Death and Dying*, 60.

23. Durkheim, *The Rules of Sociological Method*, 55.

24. Howarth, *Death and Dying*, 4, 167.

A Closer Look at Suicide

Overview

A simple definition of suicide is that it is an act of deliberately killing oneself.[25] For most of the twentieth century, scholars studied suicide as a marker of sudden, unnatural, and intended death. This has led to the assumption (which has become ingrained in society) that 'unnatural' death is associated with disorganization, whether social or personal.[26] In the modern world, some people argue that they have the right to choose to end their own life and the authority to do so, regardless of motive, circumstances, or method.[27] Suicide is not a natural and expected death; it is the consequence of an act of self-terrorism and violence to oneself. It is an unnatural and intended death and therefore meets the criteria of traumatic death.

Suicide occurs worldwide. The World Health Organization outlines the global reach of suicide as follows:

> Each suicide is a personal tragedy that prematurely takes the life of an individual and has a continuing ripple effect, dramatically affecting the lives of families, friends and communities. Every year, more than 800,000 people die by suicide—one person every 40 seconds. It is a public health issue that affects communities, provinces and entire countries. Young people are among those most affected; suicide is now the second leading cause of death for those between the ages of 15 and 29 years globally in 2012. The numbers differ between countries, but it is the low-and middle-income countries that bear most of the global suicide burden, with an estimated 75% of all suicides occurring in these countries.[28]

In 2012, suicide accounted for 1.4 percent of all deaths worldwide, which made it the fifteenth leading cause of death globally.[29]

25. World Health Organization, *Preventing Suicide*, 17.
26. Howarth, *Death and Dying*, 168.
27. Clemons, *What Does the Bible Say about Suicide?*, 13.
28. World Health Organization, *Preventing Suicide*, 15.
29. World Health Organization, "Suicide Data."

Suicide rates vary significantly between countries. The percentage of deaths due to suicide in 2008 was as follows:

> Africa 0.5%, South-East Asia 1.9%, Americas 1.2% and Europe 1.4%. Rates per 100,000 were: Australia 8.6, Canada 11.1, China 12.7, India 23.2, United Kingdom 7.6, United States 11.4, and South Korea 28.9. [Suicide] was ranked as the 10th leading cause of death in the United States in 2009 at about 36,000 cases a year, with about 650,000 people seen in emergency departments yearly due to attempting suicide. The country's rate among men in their 50s rose by nearly half in the decade 1999–2010. Lithuania, Japan, and Hungary have the highest rates. The countries with the greatest absolute numbers of suicides are China and India, accounting for over half the total. In China, suicide is the 5th leading cause of death.[30]

There is no single explanation of why people die by suicide. However, many suicides happen impulsively and, in such circumstances, easy access to a means of suicide—such as pesticides or firearms—can make the difference as to whether a person lives or dies. According to the World Health Organization's report *Preventing Suicide*, the most common methods of suicide are the ingestion of pesticides, use of firearms, and hanging. In addition to having easy access to a means of suicide, various social, psychological, cultural, and other factors can interact to lead a person to suicidal behavior.[31]

What causes suicide? There is no one factor that explains suicidal behavior. It is a complex phenomenon that results from the interaction of many personal, social, psychological, cultural, biological, environmental, and other factors. Recent research reveals the correlation between suicide and mental disorders. Many times, a person commits suicide impulsively, in a moment of crisis when he or she has ready access to a means of suicide. Acute and terminal illness, long-term life stress, and financial difficulties can also be factors in suicide.[32]

30. Wikipedia, "Suicide."
31. World Health Organization, *Preventing Suicide*, 9.
32. World Health Organization, *Preventing Suicide*, 15.

Drugs and Guns as Factors in Suicide

Margo Williams is a single mother who raised her son Matt by herself. Matt was always her pride and meant everything in her life. After Matt graduated high school in Sacramento, California, he decided to move away from his mother and home and went to college in Ukiah, California. Margo knew that Matt had some drug problems but heard that he was trying to be clean. When Margo was waiting for her son to come home during his summer break in July 1994, Matt took drugs and then took his own life by putting a gun in his mouth and pulling the trigger. He was found dead in the closet in his room. Margo recorded in her journal, "When the drugs took you into the closet, put the gun in your mouth and pulled the trigger, I also died. All that is left of me at this moment in my life is a living corpse that goes about performing daily tasks, talking, moving, unaware of much reality."[33]

Matt Williams ended his life by committing suicide. This may seem to have been a personal matter and his personal decision, but his death was accomplished with the assistance of drugs and a gun. Nowadays, drug overdoses and firearms are high-risk social factors for suicide, and they have played a role in the increase in the suicide rate in the United States. According to data from a recent National Violent Death Reporting System report, poisoning was the third-leading method of suicide, following firearm and hanging/strangulation. Seventy-five percent of suicides by poisoning were due to alcohol and/or drug overdose.[34] Based on data about suicides in sixteen states in 2010, 33.4 percent of those who had died by suicide tested positive for alcohol and 23.8 percent for antidepressants.[35] Given that drug overdoses are a factor in many suicides, simply limiting access to drugs could prevent

33. Margo Williams wrote down her feelings in a daily journal and published her one-year journal to share with others her personal pain and real struggles in the face of a violent and traumatic death. Williams, *And Then There Was One*, 16.

34. Centers for Disease Control, "Suicides Due to Alcohol and/or Drug Overdose." See p. 3 for more information on this matter.

35. Centers for Disease Control, "Suicide: Facts at a Glance 2015."

many deaths. If lethal substances are not available when people are under psychological or emotional stress and despair, their ability and opportunity to commit suicide is limited.

The Harvard Injury Control Research Center performed a review of the academic literature on the effects of gun availability on suicide rates. The report states:

> The preponderance of current evidence indicates that gun availability is a risk factor for youth suicide in the United States. The evidence that gun availability increases the suicide rates of adults is credible, but is currently less compelling. . . . Using a validated proxy for firearm ownership rates, we analyzed the relationship between firearm availability and suicide across 50 states over a ten year period (1988–1997). After controlling for poverty and urbanization, for every age group, across the United States, people in states with many guns have elevated rates of suicide, particularly firearm suicide. . . . Using survey data on rates of household gun ownership, we examined the association between gun availability and suicide across states, 1999–2001. States with higher levels of household gun ownership had higher rates of firearm suicide and overall suicide. This relationship held for both genders and all age groups. It remained true after accounting for poverty, urbanization and unemployment. There was no association between gun prevalence and non-firearm suicide.[36]

Impact of Suicide on Survivors

What makes suicide grief unique and complicated? Chelsea Ambrose, a grief counselor, argues as follows:

> There are many factors that make suicide grief complicated, but I highlight two areas in particular: guilt and the social element of suicide and mental illness-shame. The guilt a person feels overrides the grief and this can interfere with the grieving process. A person is not able to

36. Harvard Injury Control Research Center, "Firearms Research: Suicide."

grieve fully and well if they are consumed with guilt about the death. Many people feel shame about a suicide death and do not want to talk about it. The inability to talk about the death of their loved one changes the grieving process. It is very difficult to process grief if one can't talk about it.[37]

Ambrose emphasizes the importance of memorialization in the grieving process. She stresses the reality that in Western culture, other than the funeral there is typically no other family or community ritual. She feels that this is a big missing piece in our culture, but especially so in cases of suicide because of the shame or taboo of taking one's own life.[38]

Conclusion

Although traumatic death has always been one form of death and has always involved a grief process, traumatic death and loss requires a different type of grief and spiritual care than natural death and ordinary bereavement. Traumatic losses rupture the ordinary sequence of generations and defy the ordinary social conventions of bereavement. These losses profoundly overwhelm the resources of the bereaved, leaving them feeling helpless. In this chapter, I have looked at traumatic death in the U.S. social and cultural context and have examined the incidence of violence in the United States. In particular, I have discussed the incidence of suicide and explored some of the social factors that might cause suicide.

Suicide is one of the most agonizing kinds of death for surviving spouses and other family members to endure. This type of death can result in shame, anger, and guilt if family members blame themselves or are blamed by others for the death. In the next chapter, I explore psychological perspectives on traumatic grief.

---

37. Gallagher, "The Unique, Complicated Grief of Suicide," 8–9. Ambrose is a grief counselor with CareFirst, Corning, New York.

38. Ibid., 9.

2

Psychological Perspectives
on Traumatic Grief

This chapter focuses primarily on psychological perspectives on the grief connected with traumatic death by exploring the research and clinical literature on the nature of grief and bereavement. The field of grief studies has evolved in recent years as a result of the growing incidence of traumatic death. Therefore, it is important for pastors to be current in their knowledge of this literature. My focus here is on how grief and bereavement are different in the context of traumatic death compared to "ordinary" death.

MODERN STUDIES OF GRIEF

The modern study of grief began with a landmark study in the 1940s. The case concerned the deaths of 492 people on November 28, 1942, due to a fire in the Cocoanut Grove Night Club in Boston, Massachusetts. Dr. Erich Lindemann studied survivors of this tragic fire and concluded, according to Herbert Anderson, that grief is an "(a) normal response to traumatic loss, (b) with an identifiable syndrome that (c) may appear immediately after a crisis or it may be delayed, or exaggerated or apparently absent."[1] It is interesting to note that although Lindemann thought he was

1. Anderson, "Common Grief, Complex Grieving," 128.

studying normal grief, from today's perspective it is clear that he was studying traumatic grief.

According to Lindemann, the intensity of grief is determined by the nature and intensity of the griever's relationship to the lost person or object. He interviewed 101 patients. Included were psychoneurotic patients who lost a relative during the course of treatment, relatives of patients who had died in a hospital, bereaved disaster victims of the Cocoanut Grove Fire and their close relatives, and relatives of members of the Armed Forces who had died in the course of duty.[2] Through his investigation of the symptoms and reactions of the survivors, he identified common responses to grief and loss expressed during the interviews.

- The survivors experience the syndrome of sensations of somatic distress like a breathing problem, a need for sighing, and an empty feeling in the abdomen. The bereaved express feelings of guilt.[3]

- The survivors tend to respond with irritability and anger and do not want to be bothered by others at a time when friends and family are making an effort to be supportive.

- The survivors are restless, continually searching for something to do.[4]

Lindemann identified these five characteristics of grief—somatic distress, preoccupation with the image of the deceased, guilt, hostile reactions, and loss of patterns of conduct—as common signs and symptoms of grief work.[5] The duration of the grief reaction varies depending on the individual and the circumstances. When a person unexpectedly or abruptly loses an important object or loved one, the duration of the grief reaction will be longer and the grief will be harder to overcome.

2. Ibid.

3. Lindemann, "Symptomatology and Management of Acute Grief," 141–43.

4. Ibid.

5. Ibid.

WHAT IS GRIEF?

Briefly speaking, grief is the normal human emotional response to significant loss. Grief is the pain and suffering experienced after loss; mourning is the period of time during which signs of grief are shown; and bereavement is the reaction to the loss of a close relationship. One of the books that best presents grief as a response to the wide variety of losses in life comes from the pastoral care field. Kenneth R. Mitchell and Herbert E. Anderson introduce six major types of loss in *All Our Losses, All Our Griefs: Resources for Pastoral Care* (1983): (1) material loss, which is the loss of a physical object or of familiar surroundings to which one has an important attachment; (2) relationship loss, which is the ending of opportunities to relate oneself to, talk with, share experiences with, make love to, touch, settle issues with, fight with, and otherwise be in the emotional and/or physical presence of a particular other human being; (3) intrapsychic loss, which is the experience of losing an emotionally important image of oneself, losing the possibilities of "what might have been," the abandonment of plans for a particular future, the dying of a dream; (4) functional loss, which is the loss of some of the muscular or neurological functions of the body; (5) role loss, which is the loss of a specific social role or of one's accustomed place in a social network; and (6) systemic loss, which is a concept that addresses the many different types of losses in life. Grief is both universal to all and also uniquely different for each type of loss.[6]

The Experience of Grief

Geraldine Humphrey and David Zimpfer suggest that the typical grief process has five stages. First, survivors experience a sense of total aloneness and anxiety in the early stage of grief. Second, the term *risk* is used because grief work and the full resilience process may require the risk of additional pain. Survivors might experience

---

6. Mitchell and Anderson, *All Our Losses, All Our Griefs*, 36–46.

the pain of embracing the reality of the loss and its impact on them while they attempt to understand what exactly has been lost. Some will try to embrace this risk. Third, survivors might experience all dimensions of the pain, and fourth, they learn to live in the present environment that is a poignant reminder of the loss. Fifth, they experience a move toward more uncertainty through letting go of being in control of their world. Even though the loss has happened, the bereaved person needs to learn that what has been lost cannot be regained. It is time to move on, to let go, and to make new choices for the future. Lastly, the survivors move toward integration of the experience of loss, personal growth, and reinvestment in meaningful life.[7]

Grief Is Separation Anxiety

There are a couple of theoretical approaches to understanding grief's process and purposes. First, grief is best understood as separation anxiety, an acute fear in the self over the loss or threat of losing a segment of the self associated with the lost object. Otto Rank, one of Freud's earliest followers, first developed this point of view. He posited that the origin of separation anxiety lies not in the fear of abandonment or starvation but in the birth event itself. The birth event is the primal and original separation.[8]

John Bowlby, an English psychoanalyst, developed his theory of grief based on ethology, neurophysiology, information theory, and psychoanalysis, as well as on observation of animal behavior and the behavior of human children and adults in situations of separation and loss.[9] Bowlby argues that grieving developed in the human species because it served an evolutionary purpose. Bowlby focused his lifelong research on the disruption of bonding in children between the ages of six months and six years. He studied children who had been separated from their mothers for various

7. Humphrey and Zimpfer, *Counselling for Grief and Bereavement*, 37–40.

8. Sullender, *Grief and Growth*, 31.

9. Bowlby, *Attachment and Loss*.

lengths of time due to the mother's hospitalization. Children so separated showed a predictable sequence of behaviors—protest, despair, and detachment. According to Bowlby, individuals go through four phases of mourning when responding to the loss of a close relative, but these phases are not clear-cut and any one individual may oscillate for a time back and forth between any two phases. The four phases are as follows:

1. numbing, which usually lasts from a few hours to a week and may be interrupted by outbursts of extremely intense distress and/or anger

2. yearning and searching for the lost figure, lasting for some months and sometimes for years

3. disorganization and despair

4. a greater or lesser degree of reorganization[10]

It is interesting to note that in this model anger, in the form of protest, is a necessary and integral part of the grieving process. Grieving, including crying and protesting, is a type of alarm system that functions to prevent separation from the loved one. In the case of death, weeping serves to engage the sympathy and assistance of other members of the species and to rebond the mourner to a new support system. One can easily see that grief, as so understood, has held an evolutionary advantage for those humans who have grieved well.[11]

Grief Is a Process of Realization

Colin Murray Parkes, through his work with adult bereavement, proposed that "searching" is essential to bereavement. Naturally, the bereaved person looks for what is lost. Parkes understood mourning as a process of making necessary changes, adjusting to the new reality, and eventually moving toward the goal of recovery

10. Ibid., 85.

11. Sullender, *Grief and Growth*, 37–38.

and healing. "Grief is a process," writes Parkes, "of realization, of 'making real' the fact of the loss."[12] When that grieving process is complete, the new reality no longer hurts. Grief is a process of working toward that full realization. Parkes pointed out that Bowlby's theory contradicts accepted psychoanalytic views of the function of grief. These views argue that since grief appears to be a necessary consequence of loss, it must have the function of detaching the individual from the one who has gone. Yet Bowlby's theory implies that, far from promoting separation, grief has the biological function of promoting reunion. Only in the rare event of a permanent separation do the most obvious features of acute grief, pining and yearning, become gradually extinguished without reunion occurring. In Parkes's view, grief is a process of realization, of making real inside the self an event that has already occurred in reality outside.[13]

In a sense, life is an ongoing struggle with the task of loss and grief. Grief happens because we humans are relational beings with a limited time of life. There is no way to avoid grief and loss as long as we live our lives. From a biological perspective, our human life begins with the experience of separating from our mother's womb. As we grow in our life journey, we will inevitably lose people and things that we are attached to. We humans are continuously changing on many different levels throughout our life cycle. Loss is universal and inevitable throughout our life, and we cannot grow without experiencing loss. Thus, we are constantly dealing with grief in one form or another, in one degree of intensity or another.

Anderson describes the relationship between grief and loss in his article "Common Grief, Complex Grieving":

> There is no love without loss. And where there is loss, there is grief. . . . If we seek to hold on to life, we risk losing it. The deeper truth is that we find life by letting it go. Learning how [to] grieve therefore becomes a prelude to embracing that paradox at the center of Christian spirituality. The challenge is to love knowing all the while

12. As quoted in ibid., 38.

13. Glick et al., *The First Year of Bereavement*, 8–9.

that we may eventually lose what we love. Grief is a good friend for the human journey that conserves the past, teaches us about loving deeply, and builds compassion toward others who sorrow.[14]

The Grief Process

Over the years, researchers have developed many different approaches to understanding grief. One powerful view of the dynamics of grief is that it is a process. Grief work is not a static emotional event but a process that follows a series of stages. Scott Sullender introduces various scholars' grief stages theories in his book *Grief and Growth*. He notes that one of the earliest and most widely known writers to identify the stages in grief was Elisabeth Kübler-Ross, in her famous book on *Death and Dying*. She enumerated five stages: denial, anger, bargaining, depression, and acceptance. This was a pioneering piece of work, but its focus was limited to anticipatory grief, not bereavement.[15] Granger Westberg, in his book *Good Grief,* described ten steps in bereavement work: shock, expression of emotion, depression, physical symptoms of distress, panic, guilt, anger, immobilization, hope, and affirmation of reality.[16] Wayne Oates listed six stages in his book *Grief, Transition, and Loss*: shock (disbelief and numbness), sorrow, loss of meaning, anger (hostility and guilt), fear, loneliness, depression, and acceptance (resignation and peace).[17] Robert Kavanaugh described the following stages in his book *Facing Death*: shock, denial, disorganization, volatile emotions, guilt, loss and loneliness, and relief and reestablishment.[18]

Over time, the trend has been toward shorter, more generalized lists of stages of bereavement. Many scholars, however, have

14. Anderson, "Common Grief, Complex Grieving," 1.

15. Sullender, *Grief and Growth*, 55.

16. Westberg, *Good Grief*, 21–60.

17. Oates, *Grief, Transition, and Loss*, 40.

18. Kavanaugh, *Facing Death*, 110–24.

discredited the stage theory of grief altogether. They argue that an examination of the wide variety of personalities and cultures in the world indicates that there are no universal stages of grief.

Grief takes different forms, shapes, and expression depending on the griever's style and the situation. And, to complicate matters, there are many emotions other than grief that accompany the grief process. One of the pastoral theologians who has reframed this grief process into elements in a process rather than stages is Scott Sullender. In his 1985 book *Grief and Growth: Pastoral Resources for Emotional and Spiritual Growth*, Sullender lists the common elements in grief, as follows:

> Tears/Sorrow: The most obvious and, in a sense, the easiest sign of grief's presence is sadness and sorrow. Grief is a function of pain. The best medicine is to let the tears flow.
>
> Stress/Anxiety: The family who watches their loved one die a slow death is also in a prolonged state of stress. Bereavement, like all kinds of major losses, is stressful. Grief and stress are closely related.
>
> Anger/Hostility: Whenever we have been deprived, we feel angry. This anger can be expressed as self-recrimination, guilt, general irritability, revenge, over-aggressiveness, depression, and even rage. Angry feelings are a part of grief. There are two targets for anger in grief that are especially difficult to deal with for most people. First, there is anger at the deceased. The other target that is hard to be angry with is God.
>
> Depression/Despair: The standard clinical definition of depression, which dates back to Freud's work, is that depression is best understood as internalized anger. Depression is usually defined and experienced as "internalized anger." Despair, on the other hand, can be defined as hopelessness. Glenn Davidson in his book *Living with Dying* calls despair "the abandonment of hope." Maurice Farber in his book *Theory of Suicide* has called suicide "a disease of hope."

Guilt/Shame: Anger is the reverse side of guilt. Guilt assumes responsibility.[19]

Sullender's schema of the elements in the grief process is helpful and gives a framework for examining how traumatic grief might be different from ordinary grief. Various elements might be more intense or less intense depending on the nature of the loss event.

Traumatic Death and Associated Grief and Bereavement

Most scholars in the area of bereavement agree that grief is a process. This process is best understood as a journey, one that is hopefully moving toward wholeness.[20] Wholeness means restoration and recovery from hurt, pain, and suffering through the work of grief and bereavement. But the type of loss is not the only variable in grief. How a loss is experienced vary according to circumstances and the ways in which one has learned to deal with powerful emotions. For example, the sudden death of a loved one has an impact quite different from a death after a long and difficult illness. Bereaved persons, in discussing this variable, make it clear how widely feelings range. For some, a sudden loss is harder to take; for others, the sudden death of a loved one carries a small degree of comfort that the dead person did not have to suffer through a long illness. Definitely, the experience of sudden, or traumatic death as a form of violence may interrupt the flow of the grief process; it may even cause grievers to become stuck in the grief process and stop moving toward recovery and restoration.

The intensity of grief and the complexity of grieving are shaped by how the death occurs. Herbert Anderson takes this into account by modifying the definition of grief to include this factor. He suggests that "grief is a normal but bewildering cluster of ordinary human emotions arising in response to significant loss,

19. Sullender, *Grief and Growth*, 43–51.
20. Ibid., 53.

intensified and complicated by the relationship to the person or to the object lost, and by the way the person dies."[21]

Complicated or Prolonged Grief

In modern culture, family members and even trained professionals find it hard to talk about loss because it is not something that can be fixed or cured by their own efforts. Most people are not patient enough to deal with feelings or situations that are outside of their control. Many societies and communities view their highest value and goal as winning, not losing. From this perspective, a death in the family may be regarded as a failure—a failure to find a cure or make things better. In today's world, people have the tendency to deny loss. In other words, grieving is okay and acceptable, but we feel we should get over it and get ready to go back to work.[22]

Freud labeled long-term preoccupation with the lost person *complicated grief* or *melancholia*. Indeed, in current diagnostic manuals the inability to compete one's grief work is called *unresolved grief* and is defined as pathological due to the lack of resolution or closure. Unresolved grief can involve a range of emotions, but in general, according to Freud, these emotions result from the patient's refusal to relinquish the "love object."[23] There are two types of ambiguous loss: physical absence with psychological presence and physical presence with psychological absence. Both types of ambiguous loss have the potential to disturb and traumatize relational boundaries and systemic processes.[24]

Traumatic death often leads to complicated bereavement because of its intensity; the huge impact of the trauma makes it difficult for the survivors to get over it. According to trust theory, which is a rephrasing of attachment theory, trauma disrupts

---

21. Anderson, "Common Grief, Complex Grieving," 3.

22. Boss, *Loss, Trauma, and Resilience*, 4.

23. Ibid.

24. Ibid., 7.

people's basic trust and seriously impedes the grieving process.[25] In order to help those who have been traumatized by traumatic death or any type of complicated grief, it is necessary to consider a different approach to grief work.

How to Evaluate and Help People Suffering from Traumatic Loss and Complicated Grief

Sudden deaths are often more difficult to grieve than deaths in which there has been some prior warning that death is imminent. Psychiatrist Edward K. Rynearson uses the phrase *violent dying and death* to describe sudden death. According to Rynearson, there are three requisites for defining a death as violent: The act of dying is injurious, the act of dying is transgressive, and the act of dying is willful (suicide or homicide) or due to irresponsible negligence.[26] Unlike natural or expected dying and death, the story of violent death is not mutually accepted or softened. The violent dying of a loved one intensifies the feelings of helplessness that every death evokes. In the case of violent dying and death, the deceased and the family are traumatically isolated by a sudden rush of action. Family members are left out, powerless and helpless to prevent the death, and they often do not have any time to prepare for the death. Once the death has happened, this cannot be changed. In other words, "There is no opportunity to gather and create a dying story together or even to be there as the family member is dying."[27] Over the past decade, there has been an increase in sudden deaths, especially violent deaths. Certain considerations are important in working with survivors of those who died a sudden death. A sudden death usually leaves survivors with a sense of *unreality about the loss*. When the phone rings and one learns that a loved one has died unexpectedly, it creates a sense of unreality that may last a long time. It is not unusual for survivors to feel numb and walk

---

25. Sullender, "Loss, Grief and Trauma."

26. Rynearson, *Retelling Violent Death*, 21.

27. Ibid., 20–21.

around in a daze following such a loss. It is common for survivors to experience nightmares and intrusive images after a sudden loss, even though they were not present at the time of the death.[28]

How Traumatic Grief Differs from Ordinary Grief

When traumatic death happens, the shock of the sudden loss may greatly affect the survivors' emotions and the process of their grief work. If their attachment to the deceased was intense, the resulting pain will be intense. In such situations, the psyche's first response is to recoil, to deny the reality of the pain. The pain is too great, too threatening to face. Simply speaking, traumatic loss may rupture the bonds of attachment and love that bind us one to another and to other love objects. A traumatic death experience may abruptly stop our natural grieving process and healing due to its violent and powerful impact on the survivors. Survivors of violent dying are vulnerable to prolonged bereavement associated with a syndrome of obsessive thoughts and flashbacks, including re-enactments of the death as well as secondary thoughts of remorse, retaliation, and the possibility of recurrence. This intense confluence of living and violent dying causes permanent changes in the experience of living. When a violent death occurs due to human action, not only have we lost someone we love; the world we thought was safe is not. This type of violent death is a human act associated with human intention or negligence. It may occur through suicide, homicide, accident, or an act of terror. It creates a crisis for the survivors because they not only mourn the loss of the loved one but also how the person died.

According to Glick, Weiss, and Parkes's interviews with widows, some women who had lost their husbands unexpectedly reported that there was a period of numbness in which they had no feeling at all about their loss. Some cried uncontrollably, and others were overwhelmed by fear that they would not able to handle the burdens of loss and isolation. They were concerned about their

28. Worden, *Grief Counseling and Grief Therapy*, 187–88.

health, that they might have a nervous breakdown. Other widows experienced a loss of trust. The world they had lived in was relatively predictable and safe due to the presence of their husbands, but now they realized that their trust had been attacked and seriously damaged. And, very often, widows tended to experience the illusion that their husband was just on his way home or just coming to the door.[29] When the death occurred suddenly without warning, at first the widow might not be able to understand what had actually happened. At times, even though doctors and police officers informed a woman of her husband's death, she might expect that somehow what they told her would be proved wrong. On seeing her husband's dead body, she might even expect that by some miracle he would return to life.[30]

Worden, in his book *Grief Counseling and Grief Therapy*, defines sudden deaths as those that occur without warning and that require special understanding and interventions.[31] He describes some of the typical reactions to a traumatic loss:

> Tears and sorrow: Once the shock passes, the tears are very intense in traumatic grief compared to ordinary grief.
>
> Physical symptoms: As first reported by Lindemann, traumatic death intensifies the physiological stress upon the bereaved. Because traumatic death is a shock, bereaved persons are more likely to have psychotic experiences, illusionary experiences, or physical distress such as insomnia or a poor appetite.
>
> Anger and hostility: If the traumatic loss is caused by another human being, or if the death is perceived as unjust, the bereaved can experience high levels of irritability and hostility.
>
> Guilt: If death was by suicide, there may be higher levels of guilt. What should I have done, what could I have done? Why did my loved one leave me? Feelings of guilt

29. Glick et al., *The First Year of Bereavement*, 43–48.

30. Ibid., 54–55.

31. Worden, *Grief Counseling and Grief Therapy*, 187.

are common following any type of death. However, in the case of a sudden death, there is often a strong sense of guilt expressed in "if only" statements, such as "If only I had been with him."

Involvement of medical authorities: For those loved one was the victim of homicide, getting on with the tasks of mourning is difficult, if impossible, until the legal aspects of the case are resolved.

Helplessness: Another feature of sudden death is the sense of *helplessness* that it elicits on the part of the survivor. This type of death is an assault on our sense of power and on our sense of orderliness. Often this helplessness is linked with an incredible sense of rage, and it is not unusual for the survivor to want to vent his or her anger at someone.[32]

Sullender adds meaninglessness as another important element of the grief process. He writes:

Meaninglessness: Losses, suffering, and tragedies inevitably lead people to search for explanation and meaning, questioning why these things happened to them. Naturally, throughout the grief process, the bereaved develop a story that helps them to make sense of their loss. In other words, human beings have the need for a sense of meaning in life, otherwise life is meaningless—as Sartre put it, "All existing things are born for no reason, continue through weakness and die by accident. . . . It is meaningless that we are born; it is meaningless that we die." James Fowler points out that human beings can't live without some sense that life is meaningful. Humans are "meaning-making animals."[33]

Truly, we need to feel that our lives have purpose, worth, and meaning. Victor Frankl (1963) introduced the *meaning* principal, and he developed his insights into a new system of psychotherapy

32. Ibid., 188–89.
33. Sullender, *Grief and Growth*, 177.

called logotherapy (logos = meaning). He suggests that pleasure doesn't give meaning, although meaning does give pleasure.

Traumatic death appears different from ordinary grief in terms of how meaning and purpose are found in loss and suffering. Traumatic grief and loss is more intense and complex to process. The trauma is the crisis. A traumatic death leads to disruption and instability in a person's life. The bereaved find it extremely difficult to discover any meaning when they are struggling through a life crisis. Traumatic grief is often associated with feelings that life is empty or meaningless without the person who died. Shirley A. Murphy, L. Clark Johnson, and Janet Lohan wrote an article about how parents who lost their children to violent death were able to find meaning. They obtained personal narratives and empirical data from 138 parents four, twelve, twenty-four, and sixty months after their adolescent's or young child's death by accident, suicide, or homicide. The results showed that twelve months post-death, only 12 percent of the study sample had found meaning in their child's death. At sixty months, however, 57 percent of the parents had found meaning and 43 percent had not. Significant predictors of finding meaning by five years after the death were the use of religious coping and support group attendance. Parents who attended a bereavement support group were four times more likely to find meaning than parents who did not. Parents who found meaning in the deaths of their children reported significantly lower scores on mental distress, higher marital satisfaction, and better physical health than parents who were unable to find meaning.[34] Finding meaning in the violent death of a loved one is thought to be an extremely traumatic and difficult task for a victim's survivors.

PROVIDING SUPPORT FOR THE PROCESS OF RESOLUTION

What may be most helpful to offer to those who have lost a loved one due to a traumatic death is your willingness to be with them

34. Murphy et al., "Finding Meaning in a Child's Violent Death," 381.

and validate their feelings and to allow them to cry, to rage, to despair, to express all their feelings. You don't have to try to soothe them or make things better. Dorothy S. Becvar clearly reminds us of the purpose of providing emotional and psychological support and spiritual (pastoral) care to those who are struggling with a crisis and deep despair from loss and isolation. She writes:

> We may attempt to provide a sense of real support by our presence in the midst of death and dying. Accordingly, the survivors may have an awareness that they are not alone as we allow ourselves to cry with them, to express our shock and disbelief, to talk about the person who has died, and/or to share fond memories. By doing so, we may be able to contribute a sense of community as well as a sense of safety, a container for their grief, as we offer our implicit permission as well as validation for their experience, whatever it might be. Indeed, what we must not do is to try to take away the pain or talk the bereaved out of their tears. What we must do is be ready to ride the tide of emotion when a brief moment of laughter quickly dissolves into gut-wrenching sobs. We must be willing to witness the anguish not only for this loss but also for many other losses that also may have occurred. We must be able to acknowledge with the survivors what was and can never be again. And we must accept that anger and guilt may be logical responses in the initial aftermath of an unexpected death. As they are ready over time, we may then begin to think about ways in which to help the bereaved deal appropriately with, and ultimately come to terms with, their anger.[35]

What can we offer to those who want to let go of their grief, find healing, and move on with their lives? It is known that those who are grieving almost always want to recover. They seek help from all available sources. Grievers attend support groups; they read pamphlets; they buy books. After having done all these things, they are still confronted with the fact that our society is ill prepared to help them bring the grieving experience to a successful

---

35. Becvar, *In the Presence of Grief*, 58.

conclusion. Over time, the pain of unresolved grief is cumulative. Whether the grief was caused by a death or by some other type of loss, incomplete recovery can have a lifelong effect on a person's capacity for happiness.[36]

Restorative Retelling

Traumatic death forces survivors to struggle with both trauma and grief. This is a complicated and challenging task that challenges survivors' resilience. Rynearson has developed a new approach, which he terms "restorative retelling," to support those who are suffering from a loved one's traumatic death and loss. When Rynearson himself had to deal with his wife's suicide, he tried this method. He wrote about his experience, saying, "Each time that I remember and retell, I can revise and restore myself, so the darkening of Julie's dying can be lightened."[37] He argues that the purpose and power of retelling comes from reweaving a story with interconnecting strands of personal truth and meaning.[38] He acknowledges that traumatic death by itself cannot be transformed into a meaningful or courageous choice.[39] He writes:

> The violent death of a loved one differs from other traumas because it presents additional distress to the loss. Of course the relationship stops, and it doesn't. Family members continue to reach for and be touched by the persistent memory of whoever died. The relationship continues as a deep and wide remembrance of shared experiences. Memories of physical (procedural) and preverbal (episodic) experience in the relationship are as intense as verbal (semantic) memories—particularly in parents who shared nurturing experiences that were

---

36. James and Friedman, *The Grief Recovery Handbook*, 5.
37. Rynearson, *Retelling Violent Death*, 11, 15.
38. Ibid., 11.
39. Ibid., 17.

purely physical and preverbal during infancy and early childhood.[40]

During sessions of restorative retelling, Rynearson encourages naming and retelling the story of the loved one's death. He listens closely to the survivors' stories about the deceased. Restorative retelling does not just focus on the death itself; the process includes naming and retelling the vital and life-affirming experiences that encompass the deceased and that counterbalance their death.[41]

When pastors or pastoral caregivers have the opportunity to meet with family members or survivors of a traumatic death and offer pastoral support using Rynearson's approach of restorative retelling, they should be aware of a couple of important things. First, pastors should understand that it is never easy for survivors to retell the traumatic event. They might reject the idea or stop talking, even with their pastor. Pastors might have to deal with the survivor's anger, their desire to retaliate, or their feelings of devastation and despair. It is very important for pastors to first normalize the survivor's traumatized feelings and responses. Second, the pastor's role as a spiritual caregiver isn't to be a rescuer or to fix the survivor's trauma. Rather, they care for the survivor by creating a safe environment so that he or she can at last tell their story. It is an honor for the pastor to be invited to be their companion and to walk with them with on their painful journey. Rescuing, fixing, saving, or changing are not the goals of pastoral care. Instead, the pastor has the role of helping the survivor recall positive memories of the loved one and find meaningful momentum in their lives with their loved one. A compassionate heart and active listening should be the pastor's "lantern" that lights this journey with their parishioners.

Lastly, the purpose of restorative retelling is to help the survivors reconstruct a new relationship with the deceased through revising and reshaping the story of the loved one's death. The goal

40. Ibid., 87.
41. Ibid.

isn't to change the original story but to foster resilience by helping the survivors recall positive memories of the deceased.[42]

Grief Related to Suicide

Nearly 750,000 people a year worldwide are left to grieve the completed suicide of a family member or loved one, and they are left not only with a sense of loss but with a legacy of shame, fear, rejection, anger, and guilt.[43] Edwin Shneidman, viewed as the father of the suicide prevention movement in the United States, says:

> I believe that the person who commits suicide puts his psychological skeletons in the survivor's emotional closet—he sentences the survivors to deal with many negative feelings, and more, to become obsessed with thoughts regarding their own actual or possible role in having precipitated the suicidal act or having failed to abort it. It can be a heavy load.[44]

Another research-based estimate suggests that for each death by suicide, 115 people are exposed to the traumatic death. Of those, twenty-five experience a major life disruption as survivors of the loss. If each suicide has devastating effects on and intimately affects twenty-five other people, there are over one million survivors of suicide per year! Therefore, if there is a suicide every 12.8 minutes, then there are twenty-five new survivors every 12.8 minutes.[45] Pastors face the daunting task of supporting many of these survivors.

Indeed, bereaved survivors are left facing a mixture of feelings in dealing with the pain of their loss, particularly if their loved one died as a result of suicide. When suicide is the cause of death, some family members have a tendency to keep the way the person died private rather than let it be common knowledge. Family members

42. Zucker, "The Challenge of Restorative Retelling."

43. As quoted in Worden, *Grief Counseling & Grief Therapy*, 179–80.

44. Cain, *Survivors of Suicide*, x.

45. American Association of Suicidology, "U.S.A. Suicide: 2013 Official Final Data."

also have to deal with feelings of guilt and their inability to speak about the death because of social stigma. The social stigma and stereotypes about suicide in many cultures portray it as a sinful act or as representing criminal behavior that is indicative of weakness or mental illness.[46] For example, some religions do not allow the bodies of those who committed suicide to be buried on hallowed ground, nor are they willing to perform religious services in memory of the deceased. In addition, survivors, particularly close family members, may feel both anger at and a sense of being rejected by their loved one when someone they cared about succeeds in ending his or her own life. And even when resentment and rejection are not experienced, at the very least survivors may find themselves totally puzzled by the choice of their loved one and may spend years trying to figure out missed cues or other clues to what ultimately transpired. This is particularly true in the case of adolescent suicide.[47]

The following is an account of a survivor's suicide after the 1942 fire in Boston's Cocoanut Grove Night Club. This case illustrates how the survivor of a traumatic death may suffer from "survivor guilt" and end up taking his or her own life. If the death is violent, as in the case of the Cocoanut Grove fire, or if the loved one witnesses the death, bereavement can be complicated and difficult because shame, guilt, and anger make it harder for the survivor to mourn. The survivor might experience an abrupt interruption of the natural grieving process and healing due to the violent impact of the loved one's death. The traumatic death of a loved one leads to intense feelings of helplessness and isolation, plus guilt that they couldn't prevent the death. Especially when a violent death occurs due to human actions, the survivor might begin to think the world is not safe. This may result in suicide.

> A young man aged 32 had received only minor burns and left the hospital apparently well on the road to recovery just before the psychiatric survey of the disaster victims took place. On the fifth day he had learned that his wife had died. He seemed somewhat relieved of his

---

46. Becvar, *In the Presence of Grief*, 54.

47. Ibid., 55.

worry about her fate; [he] impressed the surgeon as being unusually well-controlled during the following short period of his stay in the hospital.

On January 1st he was returned to the hospital by his family. Shortly after his return home he had become restless, did not want to stay at home, had taken a trip to relatives trying to find rest, had not succeeded, and had returned home in a state of marked agitation, appearing preoccupied, frightened, and unable to concentrate on any organized activity. . . . He was restless, could not sit still or participate in any activity on the ward. He would try to read, drop it after a few minutes, or try to play pingpong, give it up after a short time. He would try to start conversations, break them off abruptly, and then fall into repeated murmured utterances: "Nobody can help me. When is it going to happen? I am doomed, am I not?" . . . He complained about his feeling of extreme tension, inability to breathe, generalized weakness and exhaustion, and his frantic fear that something terrible was going to happen. "I'm destined to live in insanity or I must die. I know that it is God's will. I have this awful feeling of guilt." With intense morbid guilt feelings, he reviewed incessantly the events of the fire. His wife had stayed behind. When he tried to pull her out, he had fainted and was shoved out by the crowd. She was burned while he was saved. "I should have saved her or I should have died too." He complained about being filled with an incredible violence and did not know what to do about it. . . . On the sixth day of his hospital stay . . . he jumped through a closed window to a violent death.[48]

Acute, sudden grief due to a traumatic death hurts deeply. The pain lasts a long time. John Hewett, in his book *After Suicide*, argues that survivors can't escape from their grief, but they can help it run its course. They must be willing to face the pain head-on, accepting the full force of it. Only by working through it, and sharing it with others, will they be able to finally let the pain go.[49]

48. Lindemann, "Symptomatology and Management of Acute Grief," 196–97.

49. Hewett, *After Suicide*, 33.

CONCLUSION

Traumatic grief is different from ordinary grief and is more intense and complex to process, leading to disruption and instability in the bereaved person's life. Usually, traumatic death occurs suddenly, without warning. In most cases, traumatic death leads to complicated bereavement because its intensity and the impact of the trauma make it hard for survivors to get over it.

Those who have lost a loved one from traumatic death typically struggle with intense emotional, psychological, and spiritual (theological) challenges. In addition, in our society there is still a stigma associated with suicide. The survivors are the ones who have to suffer the shame after a family member takes his or her own life, and their sense of shame can be influenced by the reactions of others. Another unique feature of sudden death is the sense of *helplessness* that it elicits on the part of the survivor. This type of death is an assault on the survivor's sense of power and of orderliness. Often this helplessness is linked with an incredible sense of rage, and it is not unusual for the survivor to want to vent his or her anger at someone. Lastly, traumatic grief is often associated with feelings that life is empty or meaningless without the person who died. Finding meaning in the death of a loved one is an extremely traumatic and difficult task for the victim's survivors. As I discussed in this chapter, a very helpful mechanism for finding meaning in a traumatic death is telling the story of the death and making new stories, or the process known as restorative retelling. In traumatic grief, storying becomes an important part of the healing process because it helps the survivors make meaning out of what seems like a meaningless event.

In the next chapter, I address this theme of meaning again and explore various theological perspectives on traumatic death.

3

The Challenge of Theology: Making Meaning

This chapter explores the challenges of ministering to survivors of sudden, traumatic, and violent death from the viewpoint of theology. Howard Clinebell points out that "in most crises and losses, there is separation anxiety, feelings of identity confusion, and the necessity of developing new ways to meet one's basic emotional needs."[1] Traumatic death, more than ordinary death, prompts survivors to raise questions around theodicy, such as:

- "How can a good God cause or allow such evil?"
- "Where is God in this tragic death?"
- "Why did God let my son take his own life?"
- "Why is this suffering happening to us?"
- "Where is God in our agony?"
- "In the midst of this grim reality, where can we find God's grace and mercy, power, and justice?"

These are some of the questions that people ask when they face traumatic loss. The case of sudden, abrupt, and unnatural death by violence focuses these issues sharply. I believe that the loved

---

1. Clinebell, *Basic Types of Pastoral Care and Counseling*, 185.

ones can be comforted if they can be assisted with these questions concerning a "helpless God" and/or a "cruel God." The bereaved often seek such answers from their pastor. The job of pastors is not just to provide care but also to help people find spiritual answers that are meaningful, genuine, and sensitive. Additionally, pastors are challenged to help people find God's compassionate grace and mercy in the midst of their predicament.

CASE STUDY: TRIPLETS LOST DURING PREGNANCY

In 2004, I worked as a hospital chaplain for a year at a hospital in California. This case study depicts a situation that presented itself to one of my colleagues who worked with the hospital's labor and delivery unit. He invited me to join him while he was visiting the patient. I call my colleague the chaplain here "C" and the patient "P."

One day, C received a call from the labor and delivery unit. The hospital staff requested the chaplain to visit a patient who had lost her triplets during her pregnancy. In fact, the patient herself had requested a chaplain's visit. P is a 35-year-old, single Caucasian female. Unfortunately, her boyfriend was not present when she had to face the unexpected death of her unborn babies in her womb. P said that her boyfriend didn't want to share the responsibility for the babies and that her relationship with her boyfriend had become quite distant. The patient wanted to deliver her babies and be a single parent. She identified herself as a Christian. She believed that God would have saved her babies if He were able. She prayed hard during the couple of weeks that she was experiencing medical complications. When she realized that the medical efforts and prayers had not helped to save her babies, she was deep in despair and quite angry at God. As soon as P saw us entering her room, she burst into tears and cried out to us, saying, "I prayed hard to God, but God didn't hear my prayers! My babies are gone." This young woman seemed to be desperately yearning for a miracle in the form of God's intervention to rescue her babies, but it didn't happen as she wished. She was experiencing feelings of helplessness and hopelessness. P was definitely in deep psychological and spiritual distress. She asked for any help possible from the chaplains.

Dialogue between Chaplain and Patient
P = Patient, C = Chaplain

C: I heard that something terrible happened to you today.

P: Yes, I was expecting triplets but my babies died. I just can't believe that I failed as a mom. I prayed hard to God for God to hear my prayer. I really wished that they would survive, but I feel that God didn't hear my prayer. And the worst part is that I haven't been able to say goodbye to my babies—for some reason, I haven't had that opportunity. I feel like I need to be able to say goodbye.

C: Sure, this is really hard for you. You lost your babies. This is a very difficult time for you. I am deeply sorry that you really wanted to say good bye to them but it wasn't arranged. How are you feeling now?

P: I just feel like I am in shock. I feel like God has abandoned me. I prayed so hard. You know . . . I really hoped that the babies would pull through. I just can't believe it. I was a strong believer in God. I believed that God has always been there for me, but now I am beginning to question God. Where is He?

C: Are you angry at God?

P: There are moments that I feel angry at God, but I wonder whether it is okay to be angry. Can we be angry with God? I heard that it is a sin to be angry with God, but I do feel angry at times. When I heard that I was going to have babies, I was so excited. My friends came and helped paint the babies' room, but now I feel that God is no longer there for me. I am very lonely.

C: It is too difficult for you to pray now?

P: I haven't been able to pray now. I don't even know what to pray. Most of the prayers I know reassure us about God's goodness, but it doesn't feel that way right now.

C: It seems that you are very disappointed in God. And at the same time, it sounds like you feel angry because God was not responding even though you believe God exists? Would it be helpful for others to pray for you?

P: That would be a comfort for me. Thank you so much for you thoughtful words and prayers. I wonder whether I can see my babies. I wonder whether you would be able to check for me and find my babies. I would like to hold them and to be able to say goodbye to them. If that is possible, can you give them a blessing or anointing?

C: Sure, I will try to find your babies. I can't promise you, but it wouldn't hurt to ask the medical staff. It is really important to be able to have good closure by saying goodbye to your babies. You can also pray for them. If you are okay with me doing so, I would like to pray for you and for your babies.

P: Sure, please.

In the above case, I've identified a couple of key psychological and theological (or spiritual) issues. Psychologically, P expressed her frustration and anger about her emptiness. She had a feeling of abandonment. She felt that nobody cared about her, particularly in the face of this tragic, traumatic loss. The presence of a chaplain was therefore very important and supportive in lessening her anxiety level. The patient wanted someone to care for her. Spiritually, the patient blamed God, citing the absence of God and the uselessness of God in dealing with her tragic loss. This seemed to be her biggest concern. The patient was in great spiritual distress. Her theological challenge to the chaplain can be summarized by this simple question: "Where is God in the midst of my suffering?" The key issue is neither to find the physical location of the God who was helpless to change the situation nor to blame God for not rescuing her from this horrific situation. The spiritual goal is to help the patient sense the presence of God even in times of hardship and suffering.

This patient wasn't just searching for an end to her suffering; she wanted to talk to someone and find meaning in this difficult time. P's urgent need was to meet someone who was willing to be with *her*, to listen to *her pain* due to her sudden traumatic loss and to *offer her comfort* and *validate her anger toward God*. P's statement, "I prayed hard to God, but God didn't hear my prayer," describes her deep pain and the traumatic crisis she was experiencing. Psychologically, P was facing the issue of abandonment and despair due to the loss of her triplets, and spiritually she couldn't find any meaning in her suffering. That's why she was disappointed in God. This is definitely a complicated grief situation. How can we find the "hidden meaning" in a meaningless situation? How can we find the "hidden God" in a horrific and traumatic situation?

Given the real anguish of this clinical case and keeping the various questions surrounding theodicy in mind, I now will focus on the work of two leading Protestant theologians—Gregory Anderson Love and Andrew Sung Park—and explore how their respective theologies help answer or at least inform pastors as they seek to care for those suffering from traumatic grief.

The Meaning of the Cross in a Suffering World

Gregory Anderson Love's stated purpose in his book *Love, Violence, and the Cross: How the Nonviolent God Saves Us through the Cross of Christ* is to rediscover the meaning of the cross for modern Christianity through a nonviolent and compassionate God. He begins his argument with the question, "Why is it that a violent execution becomes the center of God's plan to redeem and reconcile a fallen, suffering world?"[2] Love reflects on and thoroughly explores traditional understandings of atonement theology. In particular, he critiques the penal substitutionary theory. Briefly,

---

2. Love, *Love, Violence, and the Cross*, 12.

this theory emphasizes that Jesus' death was God's will and a way to redeem the punishment that humans deserved. In other words, the torture and death of Jesus was the direct will of God for the payment of our sin and wrongdoings against God. God had His only son, Jesus, pay the price of our punishment on the cross. Love argues that in this model God brings about redemption through violent means. Thus, God is easily misinterpreted as a fearful and threatening God rather than a merciful and forgiving God. Moreover, this theory has no saving role for the resurrection of Jesus from the dead. There are only two players in the work of salvation: humans who have sinned, bringing guilt upon themselves and alienation in all their relationships, and God, who acts through the atonement on the cross to remove the guilt of sinners and reconcile them with God.[3] Love revisits St. Anselm's traditional atonement theology, not to discover a brutal and mean God but to rediscover a nonviolent, compassionate, and loving God, which is revealed through Jesus' torture and death and the mystery of the resurrection on the cross.

St. Anselm developed an atonement theory in his book *Christ the Victor*, which he wrote the 1090s. According to St. Anselm, human beings made the decision to turn away from God. Due human's rejection of God, humans are estranged from God and are left powerless to restore harmony with God. Christianity is all about the restoration of harmony through atonement by Jesus' incarnation, life, death, and resurrection. St. Anselm's theory is often called the "satisfaction theory of atonement."[4]

Love argues that St. Anselm's theory has often been misunderstood in the history of Christianity by followers of Anselm. In this misinterpretation, sin is seen as creating a problem for God because sin insults God's dignity. So, God is angry about this, and the "God of justice" needs to punish the sinners through humiliation or by shedding the blood of the perpetrator before God will pardon the insult. But Love points out that God is not angry at the sinners. Instead, what saddens God is the breaking of the covenant;

3. Ibid., x, 40, 46, 48, 141.
4. Ibid., 198.

the breaking of promises ruptures mutual relations of trust between God and human beings. What angers God is the threat to the world God loves. But, God is unwilling to let humans destroy themselves and the world. When God sent God's only Son to earth, God's intention was not the punishment or sacrifice of God's only Son. For Anselm, God does not act to "satisfy" the divine justice by punishing the offenders or even by punishing Jesus as a substitute. God *allowed* the only Son to take on the cross because God loved the world so much that God desired to restore the old relationship (the divine–human relationship). The cross of Jesus was not the will of God; it was the will of Jesus to offer grace for all humanity. God's love was given to Jesus through human agents while he suffered and died on the cross. God's *intentional will* was for Jesus to recreate life through Jesus' death on the cross.[5]

Love proposes that God is compassionate toward sinners. God's son Jesus showed human beings God's empathy and compassion through his death on the cross. This theological view gives pastors and spiritual caregivers great spiritual insight, especially those who are continually faced with the theological question of the absence of God in the midst of human suffering and tragedy. What is Love's answer to the survivors of traumatic death and loss? Love points to three important dimensions of Jesus' incarnation. First, God became a human being like us. This comforts us in that God the Son joins us in our experience, including our experience of meaningless. God binds God's history to our own history, the meaning of God's existence to the meaning of the world's existence; this is the significance of the incarnation and the cross. In Christ, God is Emmanuel, God-with-us.[6] Second, this presence of God with and beside us in our desperate moments helps us overcome the loneliness we feel in our suffering. We find a companion in our suffering. When the randomness of catastrophes appears to make our lives cheap, we find Jesus beside us, who affirms that we are of infinite worth.[7] Jesus suffers with us as we suffer.

5. Ibid., 80, 199, 201–2, 254.
6. Ibid., 267.
7. Ibid., 248.

In his book, Love shares Nicholas Wolterstorff's personal story to illustrate his perspective on God's incarnation. Wolterstorff lost his son Eric to a mountain climbing accident. Eventually, he realized that God was present with Eric when he fell and that God also sat beside Wolterstorff when he mourned. This was a great comfort, he wrote, but it did not answer all his questions. It did not explain why God allowed the catastrophe to happen in the first place. Envisioning God falling down the mountain with Eric, God "scraped and torn," Wolterstorff asked God, "Why do you permit yourself to suffer, O God? If the death of the devout costs you dearly (Ps. 116:15), why do you permit it? Why do you not grasp joy?"[8]

Although Wolterstorff did not find an answer to his tragic reality, he experienced God's covenantal presence in a new understanding of God. What he found through God's covenantal presence was that God was with him in the experience and suffering of meaninglessness, just as Jesus trusted God's covenantal presence in his moments of doubt and struggle in Gethsemane. God not only knows our sufferings, He also suffers with us. God who made us wants to sit beside us always; God never wants to leave us. This is the heart of God, who created us and all in our world, including the meaning of all things.[9] Love shares Wolterstorff's theological reflection as his resolution of the theodicy question, reflecting on the incarnate God whose thirty-three years on earth ended on a cross.[10]

> We're in it together, God and we, together in the history of our world. The history of our world is the history of our suffering together. Every act of evil extracts a tear from God, every plunge into anguish extracts a sob from God. But also the history of our world is the history of our deliverance together. God's work to release himself from his suffering is his work to deliver the world from its agony; our struggle for joy and justice is our struggle to relieve God's sorrow.[11]

8. Ibid., 249.
9. Ibid.
10. Ibid.
11. As quoted in Love, *Love, Violence, and the Cross*, 108.

The Wounded Heart of God

Andrew Sung Park, a Korean American theologian, argues in his book *The Wounded Heart of God*[12] that Western Christian theology has understood the doctrine of sin as individual immoral choices and sinful acts against God, but it fails to represent the reality of the suffering of the victims of sin. Park points out that the Western-oriented Christian theological focus on the well-being of sinners should shift to caring for the victims of sin.[13] In order to overcome the lack of attention to victims of sin, Park suggests that the Korean concept of *han* offers a helpful clue to the theological notion of sin. In Asia, particularly in the Korean context, *han* is used to describe the depths of human suffering. *Han* is essentially untranslatable; even in Korean, its meaning is difficult to articulate. Park briefly defines *han* as the abysmal experience of pain.[14] Robert McAfee Brown interprets *han* as the relational consequence of sin; it is the scar that resides in victims resulting from the sin of those who have wronged them.[15] Park proposes a new theology for the wounded using the concept of *han*. He suggests that sin be considered "the deep wound of the heart," "frustrated hope," and the "collapsed feeling of pain."[16] *Han* is also the deep experience of the sinned against, the bitterness felt by victims of the unjust and oppressive actions of others.[17]

Park also suggests that God suffers when we experience agony and pain due to traumatic loss and grief. He argues that if what God did on the cross was perfect and we believe that Christ is the ultimate manifestation of God, then we can say that the perfect

---

12. Park, *The Wounded Heart of God*. In this book, Park compares the Asian concept of *han* to the Christian doctrine of sin.

13. Ibid., 72.

14. Ibid., 15.

15. Robert McAfee Brown was a professor of theology and ethics at the Pacific School of Religion, Berkeley, California.

16. Park, *The Wounded Heart of God*, 15–16, 20.

17. Ibid., 31.

God can suffer.[18] According to St. Anselm's theology, God is immutable and therefore we cannot imagine that God suffers, but Park argues that God suffers with human beings not because sin is all powerful but because God's love for humanity is too ardent to be apathetic toward suffering humanity. Additionally, he says that no power in the universe can make God vulnerable, but a victim's suffering breaks the heart of God. In other words, God's love for humans suffers on the cross.[19] This is how God's *han*, the wounded heart of God, is exposed on the cross. Therefore, Park argues that our image of an almighty, impassible God should be modified due to the event of God's incarnation and the crucifixion on the cross. Briefly speaking, Park argues that the all-powerful God was crucified. The cross is the symbol of God's *han*, which makes known God's own vulnerability to human sin.[20]

THEOLOGY AND MEANING IN THE STRUGGLE AFTER TRAUMATIC LOSS

Love offers an important theological insight into the reality of the suffering of God when Jesus died on the cross, especially for those who are struggling with God in their personal faith journey because they are dealing with the power of violence in the reality of traumatic death. The cross of Christ was the place where God lost God's only son in a traumatic death. God experienced the brutality and violence of traumatic death. Love reminds us that the cross of Christ was not the will of God, because God would not want to punish human sin with violence. Rather, God dearly wanted to restore the broken relationship, trust, and covenant of humans with God through the cross of Jesus, not for retributive justice but for the purpose of restorative justice. In other words, the compassionate God finally put an end to any power of violence through the cross of Jesus. God loves us as the very people we are, not in spite

18. Ibid., 121.
19. Ibid.
20. Ibid., 123.

of who we are.[21] God is shown to be a compassionate God through the cross of Jesus.

Andrew Sung Park's theological framework of the Korean concept of *han* also makes a significant contribution to Western Christian theology due to his respectful and profound empathy with those who are suffering. Western Christian theology doesn't assume that God can experience suffering and agony. Park helps us extend God's almightiness to his ability to empathize with the pain of humanity and individual suffering, especially for those who struggle with enormous pain and grief from the traumatic death of a loved one. The cross of Jesus is a perfect example of God suffering a traumatic loss and grief due to a violent death. This model opens a new door for us to find a compassionate God who understands our pain and stays with us in the midst of our pain. This is how we can understand what Emmanuel God ('God is with us') means in our daily realty. These images of God help us to remember, when we are sorrowful, in despair, and going through challenges in our life, that God is involved in the process of life rather than watching from above. God is a comforter who helps us in our trials. God weeps as we weep.

If Love were asked to provide pastoral presence and care to the grieving mother who lost her triplets in the case study discussed above, the mother whose heart was devastated by the silence of God, how would his theology help her find God's comfort and presence in the midst of a situation that felt meaningless to her? I here suggest an imaginative reconstruction of the dialogue between the chaplain and the grieving mother in the hospital, drawing on Love's perspective on the suffering of God.

21. Love, *Love, Violence, and the Cross,* 114.

Dialogue between Chaplain and Patient, Drawing on Love's Perspective
P = Patient, C = Chaplain

C: I heard that something terrible happened to you today.

P: Yes, I was expecting triplets but my babies died. I just can't believe that I failed as a mom. I prayed hard for God to hear my prayers. I really wished that they would survive, but I feel that God didn't hear my prayers.

C: I am deeply sorry for you. This is a very difficult time for you. How are you feeling now?

P: I just feel like I am in shock. I feel like God has abandoned me. I prayed so hard. You know . . . I really hoped that the babies would pull through. I just can't believe it. I was a strong believer in God. I believed that God has always been there for me, but now I am beginning to question God. Where is he?

C: Where do you think God was while you were struggling to save your babies?

P: I don't know. I feel that God wasn't with me and wasn't with my babies. How come God was so helpless when I was in such desperate need? Now I feel that God is no longer there for me. I am very lonely.

C: I hear that God seemed to be of no help when you were in great need. But what about looking at God this way? God was there with you, shedding tears and sobbing when you were struggling in your most difficult moments. When you lost your babies, God lamented and mourned over your loss right beside you. God's heart must have been "scraped and torn," as when God lost God's only son on the cross.

P: I haven't been able to pray now. I don't even know what to pray. Most of the prayers I know reassure us about God's goodness, but it doesn't feel that way right now.

C: You don't have to try to find the right prayer to say right now. God mourned while you mourned, sitting on your bed. I imagine God held your babies in God's everlasting arms, crying as you cried, beside you in your grieving.

P: That is a comfort to me. Thank you so much for your thoughtful words and prayers.

In contrast, what if Park were asked to provide pastoral care to the grieving mother who lost her triplets? How would his theology console the patient's broken heart and help her find comfort in this tragic event? The following is an imagined dialogue between chaplain and patient in the same situation.

Dialogue between Chaplain and Patient, Drawing on Park's Perspective
P = Patient, C = Chaplain

C: I heard that something terrible happened to you today.

P: Yes, I was expecting triplets but my babies died. I just can't believe that I failed as a mom. I prayed hard for God to hear my prayers. I really wished that they would survive, but I feel that God didn't hear my prayers.

C: I can't imagine how hard and difficult it is for you to go through this and don't know how I would handle it if I were in your shoes. How are you feeling now?

P: I just feel like I am in shock. I feel like God has abandoned me. I prayed so hard. You know . . . I really hoped that the babies would pull through. I just can't believe it. I was a strong believer in God. I believed that God has always been there for me, but now I am beginning to question God. Where is he?

C: God was there with you when you were suffering when you lost your babies. I believe that God suffers with you when you suffer. Your loss broke the heart of God.

P: How come God was so helpless when I was in such desperate need? I am angry at God. Now I feel that God is no longer there for me. I am very lonely.

C: God wasn't helpless, but God's heart was aching and was wounded because of your loss. I want you to know that your suffering made God feel vulnerable. God really suffered for the Son on the cross. That was not only because of God's love for the Son, but also because of God's love and affection for you. Our image of an almighty, immutable God has been changed by the Son of God's incarnation and crucifixion on the cross. God suffers when you suffer!

P: That is a comfort to me. Thank you so much for your thoughtful words and prayers.

In the end, I propose an interpretation of God that will result in better care of the bereaved and those who are traumatized by a tragic death. Throughout most of church history, the image of God has been of a powerful, almighty, omnipotent, and masculine God. Viewing God as compassionate does not mean that God is weak, helpless, and powerless. Some may challenge this, asking, "Why didn't God stop my son from taking his life?" Or, "Why didn't God stop that evil man from killing innocent people?" We need to be aware that it is all up to our choices as human beings. God is compassionate but is not responsible for preventing us from making poor decisions. The almighty God does not mean to undo our choices. Instead, God always wants human beings to make the decision to be in harmony with God. The key word to describe our relationship with God, in answer to the theodicy question, is *harmony*. When the almighty Creator made this world, everything that was created was in harmony with God. It looked perfect in God's eyes! When God's harmonious world is ruptured and our mutual covenant is broken due to human choices, God is not angry at individuals but is compassionate in restoring the harmonious world. Jesus Christ was willing to be an active mediator on the cross to bring us harmony. In the next chapter, I will explore the ministry reality in which traumatic death happens and will review, through illustrations and case studies, how pastors and pastoral caregivers deal with such crises.

CONCLUSION

In this chapter, I have explored issues related to sudden, traumatic, and violent death from several theological perspectives and have attempted to help pastors and spiritual caregivers find theological meaning in these types of situations, especially those who serve survivors facing a meaningless reality, who are unable to claim God's presence in the midst of their spiritual helplessness and despair. Traumatic death is a meaningless reality. The survivors are often suffering from despair, especially in the sense of questioning why God was powerless to change the situation. Why is God so helpless and without a voice in tragic death? I began this chapter by sharing the story of a woman who lost her triplets during pregnancy. The patient prayed hard to God, but the miracle she hoped for did not come about. After losing the triplets, she asked for a chaplain's visit. In other words, she was desperately seeking a spiritual answer, comfort, and the presence of someone who was willing to be with her in that horrific and tragic moment. Pastors and spiritual caregivers often minister to people experiencing this kind of tragedy in their pastoral ministry.

This chapter then explored the contributions of two theologians—Gregory Anderson Love and Andrew Sung Park—to these questions surrounding theodicy. First, Love's theological viewpoint would help a caregiver respond to the patient who lost her triplets during pregnancy by assuring her that God cried with her, just as God mourned over God's only son's traumatic death on the cross. And God the Son Jesus joined her in her pain, taking his cross just to be with her and to be her savior and companion. Second, Park's theological lens helps pastors and spiritual caregivers to expand their understanding of sin to include the suffering of the victims of sin. Park would have responded to this patient by expressing comfort and empathy, telling her that "God suffers with you in your agony and traumatic loss and grief. God suffers because God's love for you is so great that God cannot be apathetic toward your suffering." Park reminds us of the basic pastoral care principle that no power in the universe can make God vulnerable, but a victim's suffering breaks the heart of God. This represents a new image of a vulnerable God in the cross.

Whereas Love focuses on God's own substance (personality) as a "compassionate God" who is willing to initiate and restore our broken relationships, Park emphasizes the victim's suffering reality that breaks the heart of God and moves God to be merciful and compassionate to victims. Park makes an important contribution by expanding God's compassion to suffering victims and even to the oppressed, those marginalized by unjust systems. But his concept of *han* may not serve as an appropriate answer in every culture. For example, the Korean American social, cultural, and historical context may be different from the Korean context. Even in Chinese culture, the concept of *han* is not the same as in the Korean experience. Chinese understand the concept of *han* as "furious anger." Every culture has developed its own explanation for why people suffer.

We live in a world where violence haunts us daily in different forms and various ways. When we watch the news on television, we see homicides, suicides, and other forms of intentional death. The violence of our world is real and visible. There are millions of survivors struggling to heal from violence and the traumatic deaths of loved ones. The ancient Greek word for trauma means a "wound" or "an injury inflicted upon the body by an act of violence."[22] How can the church comfort those who have lost their loved ones and whose hearts are shattered and wounded from traumatic death and still proclaim God's grace? Serene Jones, in her book *Trauma and Grace*, raises the question, "How do people, whose hearts and minds have been wounded by violence, come to feel and know the redeeming power of God's grace?"[23]

Suffering, especially sudden, unexplainable, undeserved suffering, leads most people to question who and what God is. Is God

22. Ibid., 12.
23. Jones, *Trauma and Grace*, 8.

really in charge of the world? Does God really care? Alfred North Whitehead, a British philosopher, differentiated between the two natures of God: God as Caesar and God as Fellow-Sufferer. These terms describe the two different sides of God, which are God's transcendent and immanent natures.

- The image of *God as Caesar* is that of a Divine King, Sovereign Lord and Creator of the Universe. This side of God is above the world, apart from human history and aloof from human suffering, tragedy and loss.

- *God as Fellow-Sufferer* is another view of God, as companion, friend and fellow sojourner with each human being. This God is involved in the world and, therefore, knows intimately the pain and suffering of all living beings. This is the tender side of God, the feelings side of God, the God who listens to prayers and who suffers with and for people.[24]

Methodist Bishop Kenneth L. Carder, in his article "Why Follow a Crucified Christ?," challenges us to find God in the event of Jesus' crucifixion on the cross. He argues that God is not up in the air sitting on a throne—God humbly meets with us as a suffering, vulnerable God who will take on our burdens and sorrows in His compassion. Carder writes,

If we stop before Calvary, we misunderstand Jesus. If the disciples proclaim Jesus to be the Messiah without the cross, they will proclaim a false messiah, for Jesus' true identity can be known only at the cross. Why follow a crucified Christ? Because only a crucified messiah reveals God as a suffering, vulnerable God.[25]

This is similar to the thinking of the German theologian Dietrich Bonhoeffer, who wrote, "Only the suffering God can help." In his letters, which were later published as *Prisoner for God,* he emphasized that it is important to view the world not from the

24. As quoted in Sullender, *Grief and Growth*, 187–88.
25. Carder, "Why Follow a Crucified Christ?, 753.

perspective of an Almighty God but instead from the perspective of a suffering Christ, a weak and suffering God.

Carder continues, "The message is profound: The Transcendent One has moved into our vulnerability, our guilt, our alienation, our suffering, our death. God has claimed our weakness as a resource for divine power. God has claimed our wounds as a vehicle for our potential healing."[26] By following a crucified Christ, we can face our own vulnerability. Paradoxically, in our times of suffering and pain, we are able to recognize God's presence as a suffering God who is with us and not separate from us. God is not up on the throne but is with us here and now when we are suffering and going through a difficult time. God is a suffering God in the midst of our turmoil.

26. Ibid.

4

Overview of the Project

This chapter explains the purpose of the project I designed and conducted on the topic of providing pastoral counseling to those grieving a traumatic death. I also outline the curriculum and describe what happened in each session. I facilitated the six-week program, and each session was held in a northern California church. The sections below on each week's lesson describe the learning objective, give a summary of the lesson, and include excerpts from the discussion of the lesson, one or more case studies, and reflections on the cases.

I hope that pastors and other spiritual caregivers will find this section helpful in their caring ministries. Perhaps they can use these examples, stories, and discussion excerpts in a special workshop or as a resource to deepen the spiritual and pastoral care they offer people who are grieving a traumatic death.

Seven United Methodist Church pastors participated in the project. To preserve confidentiality, I have given them the following names: Abe, Betty, Karen, Jess, Dee, Ben, and Doug. The participants included three Caucasians (one male and two females), a Hmong male, a Filipina female, and two Korean males. All agreed to faithfully participate in the six-week program.

Each session was conducted based on the curriculum I prepared. The total length of each session was one hour. During each session, as facilitator I led a short lesson on a particular topic (10 minutes) and then each person was expected to participate in the discussion after one member presented one or more sudden death cases that they had either observed or experienced directly in their ministry (40–50 minutes). The whole group was encouraged to give their input and feedback on each case presentation. The goal was designed to help the participants learn from each other's ministry experiences with sudden death, share their wisdom, and deepen their understanding and the pastoral care they provided in their local ministry settings.

These are the topics addressed in the six sessions:

- Week 1: Traumatic death vs. natural death
- Week 2: Characteristics and patterns of traumatic death
- Week 3: Pastoral answers related to concerns about human evil and the desire for revenge
- Week 4: Ministering to those who have lost loved ones to suicide
- Week 5: Pastoral care and counseling for families after a traumatic loss
- Week 6: Helpful rituals for families

ORIENTATION TO THE SIX-WEEK PROJECT

At the initial session, I handed out disclosures, informed consent forms, and sample discussion and evaluation questions. I began the orientation session by explaining the purpose of the project. I acknowledged that pastors face challenges in responding to traumatic deaths and are expected to offer short-term or long-term pastoral care to those who are in despair due to situations of traumatic loss and grief. I raised several questions, including, What are the differences between general grief and traumatic loss? How much do we know about the dynamics of traumatic loss and grief? How can we effectively provide pastoral care and comfort to individuals or families who are grieving over a sudden loss? What pastoral care resources are available for pastors? These were the questions that had motivated me to undertake this project.

Participants

Dee (70 years old, female Filipino American pastor) has been serving a Caucasian congregation for a year and a half. Her understanding of traumatic grief and loss is that it is something that suddenly affects a person in every aspect of their being. She hasn't had a traumatic death case in her new appointment. She had general grief counseling training at seminary, but she hasn't taken any course or class regarding counseling related to traumatic death. She hopes to learn new insights, ideas, and resources for helping others.

Karen (68 years old, female Caucasian pastor) has served several churches over the last forty years. Her understanding of traumatic grief is that it is essentially the same as ordinary grief. She believes that all grief is traumatic but that traumatic grief is differentiated from other grief in terms of its unexpectedness. She personally experienced the loss of her husband a year ago, so she hopes to learn how to handle her own grief better after participating in this training program.

Ben (50 years old, Hmong American) has been serving in a cross-cultural ministry for fourteen years. The congregation is a multicultural group, primarily a combination of Caucasian, Tongan, and Hmong people. His definition of traumatic grief and loss is that it is a deep, sad form of loss. Speaking of the grief process, he mentioned that grief counseling is not needed in the Hmong culture because Hmong families have strong family bonds and connections and supportive relationships. When a death happens, all extended family members are involved in caring for the family of the lost one. Many times, the pastor has to provide spiritual care and comfort to the entire extended family, which is challenging to Ben. He would like to find a new approach to offering pastoral care to his faith community as well as his ethnic community through this course.

Jess (49 years old, Korean male) has been serving a Korean congregation. He did not have any sudden deaths in his church ministry in the last year. He noted that Koreans generally do not feel comfortable talking about their inner feelings with others, even personal feelings of sorrow and despair. In his pastoral ministry, grief counseling for his congregants is one of the challenges he faces as a Korean pastor.

Abe (65 years old, British American male) has been serving in local church ministries for forty-one years and has experienced forty-two deaths in the last two years in his local church ministry. He often finds himself objecting to concepts of definition and resisting American ego consciousness. He notices that counselors here in the United States want to be problem solvers or answer questions rather than be a person who cares for the souls of others—they are not good at soul conversation. His perspective on death, grief, and trauma is connected to the soul, but counseling professionals in this country just want to tell their clients how they should deal with their trauma and grief. He believes that the most important question should be this: How available are you to the soul and the agony of a person?

Doug (56 years old, Korean American pastor) has been serving in a local church ministry for twenty-five years. His own definition of traumatic grief is that it is a sudden loss and causes sudden damage. Last year, he experienced three cases of sudden death.

Betty (65 years old, Caucasian female) has been in ministry for forty years. Her definition of traumatic grief is that it is unexpected. Every grief is unexpected, but keeping hope alive is what pastors do, as well as giving others the courage to keep hope alive. She believes this is the job of pastors.

Week 1: Traumatic Death vs. Natural Death

Learning Objective: At the end of the session, the participants will be able to understand the nature of traumatic death and clarify the differences between natural death and unnatural death.

Summary of Lesson 1

1. Definition of Death and Grief

    Death is defined as traumatic distress and separation distress. Grief is defined as the human emotional response to loss.

    - Grief is almost universally and constantly present in us.
    - Grief is essentially the same in every person.
    - Every transition involves some degree of loss and therefore, to that extent, a degree of grief.
    - Grief is a process. While grieving, one feels as though one is on a journey—hopefully, a journey toward wholeness (full realization).[1]

2. Purpose of grief

    The essence of grief is a striving to restructure life. In bereavement, people endeavor to put life "back together." George J. Seidel of Notre Dame University says that "creativity and growth are a reordering or restructuring of chaos."[2]

    The cycle is structure–loss–chaos–restructuring.

    One cannot grow without changing. Grief is the process of healing the wound. When the grief process is completed, people say of the bereaved that they have "recovered," "been restored," or healed.

3. Sudden death and unnatural death: the specific effects of violent dying

1. Sullender, *Grief and Growth*, 7, 40.
2. As quoted in ibid., 66.

Violent dying is not only a tragic and unacceptable ending to the life story of the deceased but is carried forward as a chaotic and unacceptable ending of vitality and identity in the continuing life story of the tellers.[3]

Violent death cannot be transformed into a meaningful or courageous choice—death by homicide or accident is a transgression rather than a choice.

The 3 V's: Each violent dying occurs as a drama.

Violence: The act of dying is injurious.

Violation: The act of dying is transgressive.

Volition: The act of dying is willful (suicide or homicide) or due to irresponsible neglect (most fatal accidents are due to human error).

Summary of Group Discussion of Lesson 1

The participants were all actively serving their churches as local pastors. Pastor Abe pointed out that many professional counselors and pastors believe the myth that counseling can heal people's wounds and grief through the counselor's skillful counseling techniques. He believes that people probably don't need anyone who will listen; they want somebody to be present. He emphasized the power of presence but denied the effectiveness of the concept of sudden death grief counseling. He shared his personal story about his brother's death. When his brother, who was alcoholic and psychopathic, died, he was shocked by the sense of relief that he felt, but that didn't change his sense of deep grief. His understanding of grief is that it is just too profound to describe. Every time we try to describe it, we diminish it somehow.

Two of the other pastors agreed with this opinion. Pastor Jess shared his personal experience with a grief support group in his parish. He noticed two things. When he was dealing with a very small group of two or three people, he noticed that the grief group leaders assumed that grief is something that we can heal, but he

---

3. Rynearson, *Retelling Violent Death*, 21.

realized that the women who had been in the grief process and participated in the group were still grieving many years later. He commented that we should probably give up trying to heal our grief. He defined grief as something that we carry with us all our lives.

Pastor Dee echoed these thoughts on the dangers of thinking there can be a successful grief process. She agreed with the other pastors that we should be careful not to believe that we can somehow have control over the person who is grieving. She points out that we, as pastoral caregivers, cannot heal people's grief, but we can be there humbly with them. In other words, we may ease their pain, but their grief cannot be healed. Many pastors say that they can heal people's grief with counseling skills, but she feels that is not true.

Pastor Karen commented on her own definition of grief. She had lost her husband a year earlier. For her, there is no distinction between the grief from a regular death and from a sudden death—every death is a sudden death. She is still grieving. She also added that she believes that presence is the most important thing to offer in pastoral care, especially in a sudden death or sudden trauma situation. She said that we pastors cannot change it, we cannot heal it, but we can take it onto ourselves.

All the participants appeared to agree that presence is the most important and powerful thing that pastors and spiritual care workers can offer to those who are grieving over the loss of loved ones. Yet, they didn't identify a different dynamic in natural death vs. sudden death. My talk focused on understanding the difference between sudden death and expected death, recognizing that grief is still a demanding and hard process in both cases.

Case 1 (Father of Four Dies in a Car Accident)

This case was presented by Pastor Dee, pastor at a United Methodist Church.

K's family was on their way home around 2:00 a.m. after a vacation. K and his wife had four children. The four children were seated in the back seats. Everybody was tired, and they were falling asleep in the car. K fell asleep while driving, which caused a serious car accident. K died at the scene, but fortunately his wife and four children were still alive after the crash. K's wife called me and explained to me what had happened to her. It was still the middle of night, and I hurriedly went to her place. When I got to her house, I sat quietly beside her but didn't say anything. She seemed to be very angry and violently hit the wall in her sorrow. She and her family had left the scene of the accident and come home, with help from the police. A week later, the funeral service was arranged. At the funeral, when the coffin was brought in and placed in the sanctuary, K's wife became very emotional about her husband's death. She cried out and suddenly banged the coffin with her hands, saying, "Why did you leave me and our kids alone here?" After the funeral service, for a while I was in touch with her as her deacon pastor. She was willing to talk with me and was open to my spiritual support. She was still angry at her husband's sudden absence and his leaving her with the responsibility to take care of their children by herself. I also knew that she was depressed and was taking some medications. I was willing to listen to her and offer my presence in her time of great need. I referred her to a professional counselor for further assistance.

The group explored the implications of K's wife's acts at the memorial service. What message can we find in her violently hitting the coffin at the memorial service?

The group found three lessons in this sudden tragic death:

1. You can't prepare for such a sudden separation. It happens to you unexpectedly and is out of your control.

2. This type of sudden death hurts the rest of the family deeply because of its violence.

3. Families desperately ask for answers to the question "Why?" It is hard to understand and accept the reality of the situation. The question causes great despair, but it is hard to let go of it.

Week 2: Characteristics and Patterns of Violent Death

Learning Objective: At the end of the session, the participants will be able to identify three types of violent death situations and understand which type is the hardest to death with, and why.

Summary of Lesson 2

Three types of violent death

1. Natural disaster (acts of God)
2. Human-caused accident (unintentional)
3. Human-caused (intentional)

Which is the hardest to deal with?

1. 'Human evil'—How can some people be so evil?
2. Theological question—Why does God let evil work in the world?
3. How is the grief related to sudden death uniquely different from what is considered normal grief?

Case 2 (Couple Arguing while Driving; Three Die)

This case was presented by Pastor Dee.

A young couple was having a long argument while driving on a highway. Due to their distracting conversation, their car moved out of its lane and hit my niece's car. There were three deaths, including my niece, and many were injured. When my sister received the phone call from the police, she and her husband wouldn't believe it at first. It has been a long process for them to accept the loss of their only daughter. They were especially upset with the young people, because it seemed that they didn't show any remorse over their daughter's death, even months later. They acted like they wanted to say, "You just need to get over it because death happens every day." Those young people broke the hearts of my sister and her husband.

Pastor Betty: "This requires another layer of grief on top of the loss of the child."

CASE 3 (GROOM BREAKS OFF WEDDING AT THE LAST MINUTE; BRIDE KILLS HERSELF)

This case was presented by Pastor Abe.

I have a story about a different kind of sudden death. One day, I was counseling a couple who were planning to get married in a week. The woman was Japanese and the man was Caucasian. They had met in Chicago when the woman was a nursing student. The man suddenly broke off the relationship before the wedding date, and the woman drank a bottle of wine and then shot herself. Of course, when you hear their story, you feel and sense the violence, tragedy, and horror of it. And you may instantly want to investigate her death. Is there any racial anger in her, or what if she had not had a gun in her house—would she have taken some pills instead of using a gun to shoot herself?

Pastor Abe: In terms of grief, how is this grief different from other types of grief? Every grief is unique. As soon as you identify any category of grief, you are diminishing that grief. The worst thing that you can do is to ask how somebody died. If somebody comes to you and says, "My wife died this morning" and you ask, "How did it happen?," you are insulting the memory of the person who died. Our tradition here, and in our culture, is that we want to know. We want to have control over death. I believe that people in grief defy categorization.

Pastor Doug: I have a question on this case. You are assuming that intentional death is the hardest death. I believe that this is your assumption. As Abe points out, you cannot assume which type of death is the hardest because each grief is different.

Summary of Group Discussion of Cases 2–3

The main topic was about making generalizations about grief. The participants asked, How can we say that there is one type of death that is harder on survivors than any other?

WEEK 3: PASTORAL ANSWERS TO CONCERNS ABOUT HUMAN EVIL AND THE DESIRE FOR REVENGE

Learning Objective: At the end of the session, the participants will be able to identify the unique aspects of grief related to unnatural death (violent death) and will learn about appropriate pastoral responses for creating a space to honor the memories of the entire life of the deceased.

Summary of Lesson 3

The group discussed the following questions: If you have to respond to an individual or a family who is struggling with God in their traumatic loss, how would you share your pastoral wisdom? What pastoral responses can we find in the Bible and share with those who are grieving? What have we learned from our discussion? An outline of the discussion follows.

1. Sudden death is a crisis. The crisis is not the critical event but is a response to the event. There are three types of crisis: developmental, accidental, and traumatic (human-induced trauma and natural death). The core of trauma is *violence*.

2. Being There for Those in Crisis Reference Guidelines (adapted from Cisney and Ellers, *The First 48 Hours*)

The power of presence

- Remember that it is possible to be present with survivors physically but not emotionally and spiritually. Be on guard against getting distracted.
- Understand that being fully present with people in times of crisis is the first step in ministering to their deeper needs.
- Sometimes just being there is more powerful than anything else you can do.
- Carefully watch a survivor's nonverbal language and know when it is time to go.
- Make sure that survivors have others who can be present with them through the duration.
- Safety in times of crisis
- Understand that survivors are particularly vulnerable in times of crisis.
- Remember that survivors are likely to have a reduced level of functioning and a diminished capacity to make good decisions to protect themselves and others.
- Assess whether they feel safe and take practical steps to help them feel safer.
- Make sure that they are surrounded by people who are safe people.

Assessment and triage

- Assess the basic needs of the survivors and take practical steps to help meet those needs.
- Remember to assess any physical damage.
- Assess traumatic elements to which the survivor may have been exposed.

- Assess the survivor's perception of the critical incident. Do they see it as a traumatic event or as just a stressor?
- Assess how the survivors perceive their available resources.
- Don't assume that survivors will have adverse long-term impacts.
- Look for ways to foster resiliency in the survivors and to help them sustain emotional and spiritual growth through the adversity.
- Assess the survivors' social support systems and take steps to connect them with a good ongoing support system.

How to help: practical assistance in crisis response

- Reach out to survivors: don't expect them to ask you for help.
- Seek to serve.
- Understand that in the first forty-eight hours survivors may be overwhelmed by the critical incident and need more support, help, and direction than normal. However, make sure you don't do things they can do for themselves and further disempower them by making them feel as if they have less control.
- Assess what would be most helpful to the survivors and don't assume that you know what they need.
- Care provided should meet basic needs and be practical.
- Understand that a compassionate presence may be as helpful as anything else.
- Make sure that you do not do anything that interferes with a survivor's natural coping mechanisms.
- Get permission from the survivor before helping, but see if there are ways that you can help coordinate care within the faith community for immediate and ongoing support.
- When there is an unmet need, find and coordinate a link for them with a referral for support or services.

Telling the story

- Seek to be a great listener.
- Learn to ask gentle questions, and listen more than you talk.
- Understand that it is important to establish a connection and a safe environment before survivors may be ready to talk about their situation.
- Be available to talk when survivors need to talk.
- Be prepared for strong emotions that survivors may need to express, but don't assume that the absence of this is an indicator of negative coping.
- Remember that survivors may say a lot of things from an emotional place that they don't really believe when they are working through their trauma and loss.
- Be accepting and non-judgmental.
- Understand that there is a broad diversity in the amount that people need to talk about their situation.
- Balance talking about the critical incident with normal conversation.
- Understand that a survivor's story related to a critical incident is likely to continue to change as his or her perspective changes throughout life.

Hope in times of crisis

- Remember that hope in the early aftermath needs to focus on something simple and concrete.
- It is better to help survivors discover hope than to lecture them about what they should hope in.
- Understand that it is natural for people to lose hope when life becomes overwhelming.
- Connecting survivors with other survivors who have experienced similar crises and who are emotionally healthy can be helpful.

3. The way to heal the wound from grief is to go from meaninglessness to meaning.

The essence of grief is a striving to restructure life. In bereavement, people endeavor to put their lives back together. The cycle is: structure–loss–chaos–restructuring. One cannot grow without changing. Grief is the process of healing that wound. When the grief process is completed, people say of the bereaved that they have recovered, been restored, or healed.

4. Goals and tasks in the aftermath of violent death: How to discover or make meaning

The violent death of a loved one differs from other traumas because it presents additional distress to the loss. Of course, the relationship both ends and does not end. Family members continue to reach for and be touched by the persistent memory of the person who died. The relationship continues as a deep and wide remembrance of shared experiences. Memories of physical (procedural) and preverbal (episodic) experiences in the relationship are as intense as verbal (semantic) memories—particularly in parents who shared nurturing experiences that were purely physical and preverbal during infancy and early childhood.

Violent dying needs a restorative retelling. The continued retelling of a violent death is fundamental to anyone who loved the deceased. The purpose of counseling and grief is to help learn how to balance oneself above the meaningless void of violent dying, but counseling cannot promise a precise answer. Realigning with the violent dying of a loved one is a dynamic balancing act, like walking on a tightrope across an abyss by transcending fear and taking small, determined steps toward the end of a rope that stretches into the future.

5. Normal process of healing the grief wound

Sudden death vs. normal grief:

- There is no time to say "goodbye"

- The why factor: Why me? Why has God abandoned me? (How can caregivers help families face this challenge?)
- Families may want to seek revenge or may become obsessed with examining the details of the death

6. Caregiver responses in situations of trauma
   (by Daniel S. Schipani)

Do say:

I am sorry this happened to you.

You're safe now (if the person is indeed safe)

I'm glad you're talking to me now.

It wasn't your fault.

Your reaction is a normal response to an abnormal event.

It must have been upsetting/distressing to see/hear/feel/smell that.

You're not going crazy.

Things may never be the same, but they can be better, and you can get better.

Your imagination can make a horrible reality worse than it is.

It's okay to cry, to want revenge, to hate, and so forth.

Don't say:

I know how you feel.

I understand.

You're lucky that you're alive.

You're lucky that you were able to save something.

You're lucky that you have other children/siblings and so forth.

You are young and can go on with your life / find someone else.

Your loved one didn't suffer when he/she died

She/he led a good and full life before he/she died.

It was God's will.

He/she is better off / in a better place / happier now.

Out of tragedies good things happen.

You'll get over it.

Everything is going to be all right.

> You shouldn't feel that way.
> Time heals all wounds.
> You should get on with your life.[4]

7. Pastoral Responses

Lam 3:55–57:

"I called on your name, O LORD,
from the depths of the pit;
you heard my plea, 'Do not close your ear
to my cry for help, but give me relief!'
You came near when I called on you;
you said, 'Do not fear!'" (NRSV)

Matt 5:4 (the compassionate God):

"Blessed are those who mourn,
for they will be comforted." (NRSV)

Case 4 (Loss of Triplets in Pregnancy)

The case presenter was Jeong Park, the facilitator of the six-week project. He presented a verbatim of pastoral care counseling from his chaplaincy work at the hospital. The patient was a 35-year-old, single Caucasian female. Unfortunately, her boyfriend was not present when she had to face the unexpected death of her unborn babies in her womb. The patient said that her boyfriend didn't want to share the responsibility for the babies and that her relationship with her boyfriend had become quite distant. The patient wanted to deliver her babies and be a single parent. She identified herself as a Christian. She believed that God would have saved her babies if He were able. She prayed hard during the couple of weeks that she was experiencing medical complications. When she realized

---

4. Schipani, "Pastoral Care in Crisis Situations," June 23–July 4, 2014 class lectures.

that the medical efforts and prayers had not helped to save her babies, she was deep in despair and quite angry at God.

This is the same case that I presented earlier in chapter 3, in which the original verbatim (written record of the dialogue between patient and chaplain) was paraphrased and reconstructed several times in order to highlight particular theological issues in this traumatic loss and death situation. The following verbatim reflects the actual dialogue between chaplain and patient, so there are some differences between this version and those in chapter 3. In week 4, the group used the following verbatim as a case study. They read out loud from a script of the verbatim.

Dialogue between chaplain and patient
P = Patient, C = Chaplain

P: All my babies are gone now! [Her voice is trembling in anger and frustration.] Nothing is left in my life! [The father of the triplets was not present at this time. Later, she shared about her struggles in her relationship with her boyfriend.]

C: I am so sorry for your loss. This is terrible. I can't imagine how you are handling this difficult time.

P: I have prayed to God to save my babies day and night. But God didn't hear my prayers. Now I feel that God doesn't care about me.

C: I understand your feelings. You must be angry at God.

P: Yes, I am angry at God. How come this happened to me? Why me? Why didn't God respond to me at all?

C: Sometimes, we do not understand God's will and plan for us. Do you know the story of Job? In the Bible, Job was a righteous man, but he had to suffer and endure many challenges without any clear reason. He didn't understand why God allowed him to go through all that. He must have been quite frustrated and angry at God. I am sure that you have the same feeling now.

P: I feel God is so mean and brutal to me. My life has been destroyed. There are no more things left to lose in my life. [The patient is sobbing.]

C: [presenting a Bible to the patient] I hope that this Bible will bring you some comfort while you are going through this difficult time. Please let me know if I there's anything else I can do.

P: Thank you, chaplain!

An excerpt from the group discussion of case 4 is as follows.

Pastor Doug: One thing about grief counseling, as our discussions have made clear to me, is that (1) the counselor should not try to lead the counselee, (2) we cannot predict/expect the outcome of the counseling, and (3) counseling should flow naturally, without any artificial, external influence.

I did not particularly feel attracted to the idea of referring the present struggle to the biblical figure of Job as a helpful model or an example. By introducing Job, it appears to me to be suggesting that the counselee should assess his or her situation in terms of relative degrees of suffering, in deference to the preponderance of the suffering the biblical figure had borne "stoically."

I personally feel that the examples of suffering figures in the Bible are not there to inform us how far we can and should go in our sufferings. I am not convinced that such an example would be effective in real life because there is no connection between the biblical figure and the modern suffering person. I feel that Jesus' approach, so to speak, is more appropriate: laugh with those who are laughing and cry with those who are crying. I feel that sharing compassion and grief is what the person needs rather than an example of how a biblical figure overcame grief, etc.

The grieving person should dictate how grief-bearing takes place, not the counselor. Some may want to be surrounded by people; others may want to be left alone. It is up to the counselor to fine-tune his or her sensitivity to discern these needs and be present in the appropriate way. I would say that grief counseling is an art, having no firm, established formula.

Case 5 (Suicide of a Nineteen-Year-Old Man)

This case was presented by Pastor Betty, a United Methodist Church pastor.

It is quite a different experience living on the coast. People often move to the coast because they don't really want to deal with others. In my observation as a pastor there, there seems to be many introverted people living on the coast. It is hard to perceive the great need for community support among families on the coast. I experienced several cases of suicide among young, middle-aged, and older people that challenged local clergy to create a new ministry to help the community. Even though there is a volunteer hospice group, we realized that we needed a new group to work together (as a pastoral group among many faith-and non-faith-based people) to find ways of ministering to folks on the coast in times like those.

The particular piece which stays with me is the death of a nineteen-year-old boy who took his own life on a beach at 5:30 in the morning. This is a case in which the community responded by coming together and struggling with the loss of this young man for over five or six years. When I was appointed to a church there, and had served for six years, people were still coming together each year on the beach to grieve his death, to comfort and encourage one another. I will call him Derek, a very bright young man who was definitely not challenged by the school system there but was connecting with the home school group and enrichment class. He and other home schoolers used to meet during weekdays at our church, as many home schooling groups have their schooling at the churches. They find connections there, too.

When Derek graduated from high school, he picked up a newspaper route. He worked three hours every night. There may have been time alone on the road, time to be with his own thoughts and time with his real struggles. The situation he had to face was that his parents had split up and his sister was preparing to open a local business. Family attention was only given to his sister starting the business, and his mother was healing herself after the split-up with his father.

One day, after he had finished his route early in the morning, he went to the beach and took his life with a gun. That happened on a Saturday morning, and slowly, that Sunday night, we were able to organize a group of people who just needed to unpack that. Just to be together and just know that they weren't alone . . . his family wasn't alone. So we met on the beach and held candles and just told stories about him. We didn't try to explain anything but just shared with his friends and family things that we appreciated about him, who he was, stories about when I first knew him when he was five years old, and whatever stories others wanted to share. Then they met together in a variety of places week after week.

Family and friends continued to struggle with the loss. Every year, a number of people came to the church to join a special Christmas service, which is like a Taizé prayer format and a place where people come and read their prayers. Sometimes people stood and shared a few words from their hearts to lift up in prayer. It wasn't anything to fix, but a place to remember people, especially young men and women who took their young lives. We shared how we, as a community, can help young people appreciate their lives and create places for them to lay down their burdens and speak their truth. We started forming circles for boys and girls and circles for kids who were not in high school anymore, especially those who were in between seventeen and twenty-two years old. We were aware that those young people are often abandoned and excluded in many ways because there isn't any place for them to go to belong, to share their struggles, and to be loved. So the community began to see and talk about ideas and plans to care for young people in the town so that we might try not to be hermits on the coast but to become community for one another. That conversation is still going on. It was a powerful experience to notice people's awareness of the need to build a spirit of community through a young man's death.

We may learn a lesson from the Hmong people about the meaning of community in difficult times of grief. They have services not only in funeral homes, but they also have services at their homes.

The pastors reflected on this case as follows.

Pastor Ben: My cousin passed away. The timing of the funeral really depends on when the funeral home is available, and it also depends on how and where relatives will be coming . . . in any event, it takes time. In my cousin's case, he passed away on a night in July, and on that night I, as his cousin, hosted a memorial gathering for the community. When the community people came, we provided the hospitality. Everybody talked about their memories of my cousin. Just being there (even though they did not directly talk to the children and family), we were inside the house, and outside the house, and people were making noise. This happened not only the night that he passed away, but every night until two weeks later, when we took his body to the graveside, and after that night, we went to his home and followed up with a big feast a few nights later. This kind of conversation is designed to help the family who is grieving over the loss of a loved one.

Guest from the Conference District: It is interesting how other cultural perspectives are working because in my culture (White Anglo-Saxon), we want to get him in the ground and get away. . . . I am serious, that's the White thing, and then walk away. I have noticed that many Asian cultures have different ways in which to remember and support one another.

Pastor Ben: In my role as one of the family members and also as a pastor, it was difficult for me. I didn't want to confuse people with my role as a pastor, but I was there almost every night, providing hospitality.

Pastor Doug: One thing that came across loud and clear was the cultural norm. We are from differing cultures, and our world perception has been shaped by the cultural norms. Our expectations and the way we behave in our most trying times vary, depending on culture.

This means that the counselor brings his or her own assumptions about how one goes about dealing with grief counseling. Again, the counselor must follow the dictates of the situation and the culture of the people whom he or she intends to serve. The counselor must be familiar with the cross-cultural variations in how people deal with a traumatic situation. Our guest's assessment of his own cultural norm is a good start for good, effective counseling. One should be aware of one's own culture and understand the counselee's culture, as well.

Another thing about grief counseling, or dealing with grief, is the knowledge that the community cares. As Pastor Betty's presentation makes clear, it is the community response and the long memory that might bring eventual healing and sharing of the burden. The counselor may offer personal counseling, but it is more effective when he or she can be the catalyst to bring the community together to share the grief and the memories of the departed. The grieving family is healed by the presence of the community and the knowledge that the community knows them, cares for them, shares their burdens, and remembers them.

WEEK 4: MINISTERING TO THOSE WHO HAVE LOST LOVED ONES TO SUICIDE

This session was held August 19, 2014. Lesson Objective: At the end of the session, the participants will understand three types of grief, including the grief associated with suicide, and will understand how grieving a suicide is different from normal grief. At the end of the session, the participants will know three pastoral approaches to helping people grieving due to a death by suicide.

Summary of Lesson 4

These are the questions the group discussed in this session:

1. Is suicide bereavement different from mourning after other types of death?

2. What pastoral ways can pastors (pastoral caregivers) provide help to those grieving a loss due to suicide?

3. What have we learned from our discussion?

The lesson addressed how to minister to those who have lost a loved one from suicide, three distinctive aspects of suicide-related grief, and how grief associated with suicide is different from normal grief.

Suicide bereavement is distinct in three significant ways:

- The thematic content of the grief
  These special themes of suicide bereavement manifest themselves in three broad areas of grief response. First, numerous studies have found that survivors seem to struggle more with questions of meaning-making around the death ("Why did they do it?"). Because suicide is self-inflicted and violates the fundamental norms of self-protection, survivors often struggle to make sense of the motives and frame of mind of the deceased. Second, survivors show higher levels of feelings of guilt, blame, and responsibility for a death from suicide than from other types of death ("Why didn't I prevent it?"). Occasionally, survivors feel that they directly caused the death through mistreatment or abandonment of the deceased. More frequently, they blame themselves for not anticipating and preventing the actual act of suicide. Third, several studies indicate that survivors experience heightened feelings of rejection or abandonment by the loved one, along with anger toward the deceased ("How could they do this to me?").

- The social processes surrounding the survivor

  The most comprehensive review to date of research on suicide survivors did not address the issues of the impact on the social network on survivors. Yet there is considerable evidence that survivors feel more isolated and stigmatized than other mourners and may in fact be viewed more negatively by others in their social network.

  "Self-stigmatization" can be an issue for survivors of suicide. For example, one study found that suicide survivors worried more about what others really thought of them, felt uncertain about how to act and what to share with others, and believed that community members were likewise uncertain how to behave around them. Strikingly, in this study 76 percent of those bereaved by accidental death reported that the changes in social interaction were positive in nature, compared with only 27 percent of suicide survivors.

- The impact suicide has on family systems

  The pre-existing interactional patterns of some families in which a suicide occurs may be different from other families, and the suicide itself may contribute to dysfunctional family dynamics. Although by no means present in all cases, there is evidence that families of many suicidal people (particularly suicidal children and adolescents) show more disturbed family interactional styles and increased disruptions of attachments when compared with families without a suicidal member.

  Also, there is a heightened risk for additional family suicide. Suicide bereavement is an unusual form of mourning experience because losing a loved one to suicide may elevate the mourner's own risk for suicidal behavior and completion.[5]

---

5. Jordan, "Is Suicide Bereavement Different?"

Case 6 (Various Suicides)

This case was presented by Abe, pastor of a United Methodist Church.

The heightened risk thing, I think it is really important, and we've seen it with Robin Williams. It's not just a family. It's very visceral for all of us when we hear about suicide. We imagine ourselves in their place. And that is why there was a greater number of calls to suicide hot lines after Robin William's death than ever before.

In April 1996 my father had a series of small strokes, and from that, his two basic loves in life he could no longer do: golf nor drive a car. My mother had been his mother really for all of his life—he was an orphan. In July, his wife and caregiver for all of his life, she was always looking out for him and caring for him for fifty-some years, she received a terminal cancer diagnosis. I believe my mother was just devastated that my father was going to have to be her hand-and-foot nursemaid and have to do everything for her. I believe she deliberately chose not to go to the doctor, and she died the following January. So I think she committed suicide, in one sense. I see a lot of deaths with a suicidal component. I would guess thirty to forty suicides I've known, and they can be so different. When I came to California I did a memorial service for a family of four who took their lives at Jonestown. I had believed in all the stages of grief from Elisabeth Kübler-Ross at that time.

The first one was my older brother Chris, who was alcoholic and sociopathic. My brother had a crisis and was on life support, and within three hours he died. He was fifty. Actually, my overwhelming honest response was one of sheer relief. There was grief before that day, though, because he was bright and very able, and everything fell apart. He couldn't function. Very hard relationship for me; the reality of my brother was very hard. His death was liberation from that for me. So, there are lots of different kinds of experience. . . .

A woman who had been around our church became notorious in southern California when she committed suicide by walking into the ocean, taking three children with her, and two were saved. In Japan, when you are just so destitute, nothing is left for you and the shame is too much for you, suicide is acceptable, even taking your children with you. Really shook up the congregation. I think I do understand.

In all the issues of suicide and grief, I worry about bringing intellectual concepts to them. I think there's a sense in which death finds us, the soul is like that. The soul is not something we conceptualize or understand, as in the Western way. The soul is something that happens to us, that has its way with us. We need to embrace it, to claim it and live it authentically somehow.

A few months ago here, an older couple in the congregation saw a walker in the thrift store, bought it. They came home and set it up by the car. The man, who had certain issues with his mind, sat on it. It had wheels on it and rolled backwards down the driveway, a freak accident. He cracked his skull and died within twenty-four hours. Very sudden, totally unexpected.

The widow has been on my mind a lot. I didn't sense that her grief was any different from any other widow's, though this was a sudden death. Some people are more ready than others. This grief didn't have anything to do with the circumstances of the death. Even when you know somebody is dying, and it's expected, it always surprises emotionally. The widow's sense of her grief was sudden, totally unexpected in this case. But, emotionally, all death is sudden.

Excerpts from the group discussion of case 6 are as follows.

Pastor Abe: The survivors' world is upside-down.

Pastor Dee: If I am approaching the person who is grieving, it would be better for me if I could read their mood, then I can appropriately respond to them. I cannot judge them. All I could do is laugh with them or cry with them. But I think judgment is the wrong thing. I would want to reassure them that there is not eternal condemnation because they kill themselves.

People from the outside say suicide is a choice, but there may not have been a choice for that person. Maybe that was the only way. I would be making a mistake if I were approaching with the assumption that that person made a choice. Maybe they had no choice.

Pastor Dee: I had a friend; she was like a sister to me. It was very close to home when I heard; it was disbelief, then grieving. Then it really just changed me, whenever I go over the Golden Gate—her daughter jumped off that bridge. She was battling a mental illness. . . . She quit working to stay home with the child. When I heard this, we went over to the house.

Pastor Jeong: Do you recall your conversation with them?

Pastor Karen: We just listened; they wanted to talk. We were there for two hours, just listening to her talk and empathizing. Happened in August, waited until her birthday in February to have the memorial. In between that time, we were just embracing them and kept talking with them. When I'd ask her how she was doing, she'd say, "Slow-slowly."

Pastor Jeong: Sometimes we wonder what to say in that situation [the memorial service]. No words.

Pastor Karen: What we need is to be surrounded with support, to hold each other. You don't need to say anything.

Pastor Jeong: Obviously, we have to prepare a homily.

Pastor Karen: It's so hard to put things together for an occasion like this.

Pastor Abe: Grieving for a long time is problematic for people. But after the memorial I ask them to write down what happened, the story, and scriptures that helped them. There's always something that . . . I believe it's my priestly duty to do that, to make holy what is feeling very unholy.

WEEK 5: PASTORAL CARE AND COUNSELING FOR FAMILIES AFTER A TRAGIC LOSS

Lesson Objective: At the end of the session, the participants will know pastoral ways to help families find hidden meaning and the value of life in the midst of situations of tragic loss and death.

Summary of Lesson 5

1. Grief is defined as the human emotional response to loss. Grief is also a process. The essence of grief is a striving to restructure life. Grief is the "redefinition of self." A person is not able to grieve fully and well if they are consumed with guilt about the death. For example, in the case of suicide, many people feel shame about the death and do not want to talk about it. . . . The inability to talk about the death of their loved one changes the grieving process. It is very difficult to process grief if one can't talk about it.

    Grief in the words of C. S. Lewis following the death of his wife:

    > Tonight all the hells of young grief have opened again; the mad words, the bitter resentment, fluttering in the stomach, the nightmare unreality, the wallowed-in tears. For in grief nothing 'stays put.' . . . Everything repeats. Am I going in circles, or dare I hope I am on spiral? But if a spiral, am I going up or down it?[6]

    Acknowledging that there is no timeline for grief and that everyone experiences grief differently is the only way that one can come to a reconciliation of one's grief.

---

6. Lewis, *A Grief Observed*, 46.

2. The importance of memorialization in the grieving process . . . there's a funeral and nothing else in Western culture.

3. Pastoral support: suggested scripture readings

    a. Rom 8:38–39:

> "For I am convinced that neither death, nor life, nor angels, nor rulers, nor things present, nor things to come, nor powers, nor height, nor depth, nor anything else in all creation, will be able to separate us from the love of God in Christ Jesus our Lord." (NRSV)

    b. 1 Cor 15:42–43:

> "So it is with the resurrection of the dead. What is sown is perishable, what is raised is imperishable. It is sown in dishonor, it is raised in glory. It is sown in weakness, it is raised in power." (NRSV)

    c. 1 Pet 1:23:

> You have been born anew, not of perishable but of imperishable seed, through the living and enduring word of God." (NRSV)

    d. Isa 53:4–5:

> "Surely he has borne our infirmities
> and carried our diseases;
> yet we accounted him stricken,
> struck down by God, and afflicted.
> But he was wounded for our transgressions,
> crushed for our iniquities;
> upon him was punishment that made us whole,
> and by his bruises we are healed." (NRSV)

Alan Wolfelt proposes six central needs of mourners rather than stages of grief. These six needs are:

a. Accept the reality of the death.

b. Let yourself feel the pain of the loss

c. Remember the person who died

    d. Develop a new self-identity

    e. Search for meaning

    f. Let others help you—now and always[7]

4. The pastoral caregiver's role

    Jer 29:14:

    "I will restore your fortunes and gather you from all the nations and all the places where I have driven you, says the LORD, and I will bring you back to the place from which I sent you into exile." (NRSV)

    With the love of God and the hope of resurrection, pastoral caregivers can hear, honor, and encourage the practice of lament. Encourage an authentic communication with God, born out of deep anguish in protest of their pain and their position toward hope.

    a. Provide pastoral care based on the principle that the survivor is experiencing profound grief and trauma, complicated by guilt and the stigma of shame. These all hinder the grieving process. Show them unconditional love, modeling Christ's love.

    b. Reach out to survivors on special days that are very difficult for them: the birthdays of their loved one, holidays, the anniversary of their loved one's death.

    c. Be very careful of your language around survivors. Do *not* say things like, "Well, tomorrow will be a better day" or "I know exactly how you feel because once I had a dog that died" or "Well, at least Susie is in a better place now." The best thing to say is "I am sorry" or to say nothing at all and just give a hug if appropriate.

Group Discussion of the Pastor's Role

Pastor Jeong: I come from Korea, so maybe I'm not the right person to speak about Western culture, but here, when someone dies, as ministers we do the graveside service, and then that's it, not

7. Wolfelt, *The Wilderness of Suicide Grief*, 79–86.

excellent pastoral or spiritual care, not many things we do after that.

Pastor Dee: I disagree. I think what you are speaking of are the rituals and gatherings in Asian cultures. Big gatherings. In this country, there's not such big gatherings. I'm married to a Caucasian, I see a lot of expression of grief. We don't see it as much, but it is contained in the immediate family, whereas back home in the Philippines, the rituals are very big and involve the extended family, so everybody wants to be in there

Pastor Jeong: My point is, we need rituals to express grief. As part of a lifelong struggle, to support the family who has lost a loved one . . . how can we help besides the funeral or graveside service? Importance of memorialization, might be difficult to remember because there is such a hole in my heart, and I feel shame to share my grief. The memorial service is inadequate by itself to minister to a grieving family. People may just keep their grief to themselves but it's important to keep remembering, pastors can keep remembering, perhaps sending cards to the bereaved, reach out to survivors on important anniversaries that are especially difficult for them.

We must be careful of our language around survivors, not to say things like "Tomorrow will be a better day "or "Susie is in a better place now." We need to be very mindful of how much they are in anguish. We need to be mindful of our choices of scripture in services; it may not be relevant to a sudden death situation. Perhaps a lament in Scripture, or "nothing can separate us from the love of God" [Rom 8].

C. S. Lewis's lament about losing his wife: "Tonight all the hells of young grief have opened again . . . the nightmare of grief . . . for in grief nothing stays put, everything repeats . . . am I going in circles . . . am I going up or am I going down?" It's important to remember, verbalize, that really helps. It's an opportunity to reconstruct the story, to recall the memories of this loved one. It really helps to simply recognize the grief, so it doesn't remain just the bitter reality, and use the opportunity to remember the person who is lost.

Pastor Betty: Don't tell people what they should be feeling, how they should grieve. But help them move beyond that. I've got a quote here: "There is a gift here . . . the gift is real and precious and you can find it if you choose." This is the search for meaning. Without this process of searching for meaning, grieving is just a miserable repetition.

Pastor Betty: It's part of the "why" question, the meaning.

Pastor Jeong: Our role is not to find answers for them but simply to be there to listen, hold hope that they discover for themselves; eventually God will comfort their hearts.

Pastor Abe: Grieving isn't something to be avoided, it is something that you have to act on, and then move on.

Pastor Jeong: It's a lifelong process.

Pastor Karen: What does it mean to "develop a new self-identity?"

Pastor Jeong: To reconstruct our life after a sudden death, not be a griever for all time, but to move on to something else, even though we acknowledge our loss, we are not where we were, and we grow; we do not stay where we were.

Pastor Abe: We are missing something when we deny that we are grieving. If people are too quick to celebrate a life without recognizing the grief, then we are actively resisting or denying that we are grieving. If someone dies, my first business is to grieve. To be too quick to celebrate is inauthentic.

Pastor Betty: At my previous church I could celebrate, in order to accept the death . . . it's individual, depends on who the [deceased] person was. I needed that celebration. It helped me see what was. Sure, I had to grieve. . . . But I can remember the good things. But then I could also move on. I would be wasting that if I could not celebrate that and then move on. We're not into death, we're into resurrection. I needed that celebration to help me reaffirm my hope and my future.

Pastor Dee: In my culture, people would ask, How can you laugh or celebrate, when she just lost somebody? That is cultural.

Pastor Jeong: Without acknowledging grief, where we are, then we . . . grieving is helping us to move on, we need to let go or we miss what is or our life is really hard. Traumatic loss is really hard . . .

Pastor Abe: I really don't like these "six needs," I *hate* the language of stages. I think it's really important what you write, that the central reality of grief is that you want to be very present there with the person and enable them to stay present. In Gestalt therapy they write about staying at the impasse; it is only when you really feel the discomfort of where you are, that's where the pastoral role should always be. Right now is when it is really important that they experience exactly where they are right now and they stay there. Then you are able to move into healing.

Our congregation is being gripped by the imminent loss of a woman with terminal cancer. She is adored by the members of this congregation. Everybody in the leadership is immobilized. Everybody has got themselves caught up in her reality. I find myself running into many people who need to just talk about this. The grief already is huge and she hasn't even died yet.

In the African tradition you have memorial services at thirty days, ninety days, six months, twelve months. . . . Over one hundred thousand people were at a prominent chief's funeral in Nigeria. At twelve months, over four hundred came to a regular service at our church. As the congregation was going out, a little old lady who had lost her husband eight years ago said, "When you were saying the prayers for this chief from Nigeria, I suddenly realized you were praying for *me* and for my husband." This is the reminder that we need the rituals.

Pastor Dee: Back home [in the Philippines] the service can be for someone who died twenty years ago. Returning there, it can seem like too much, *nine days* of services. But in my extended family here, we do a memorial on anniversaries of deaths

Pastor Betty: Here, nobody wanted to do anything.

Pastor Jeong: Perhaps have one day each year—like for all the saints—ask each mourner to bring their own candle.

Pastor Dee: Other special remembrances each person brings—we had bubbles [balloons?] with memories of each person who died. I got a call from someone who I had ministered to in her loss twenty years ago. She said, "I just wanted to hear your voice because it reminds me of my dear one and coming through the loss. I am very grateful." We are that to these people who grieve.

Pastor Abe: It's the priestly function, you are a mediator of the grace of God, just by the sound of your voice, there's nothing to say necessarily.

Pastor Betty: Grief can hit you at any time and you can come apart. It would be so helpful to have someone who understood this that I could talk to. Who do you call? There's nobody to call to share with who understands. I do that for other people. It's really hard for me to ask anyone, everyone's so busy. The idea is, "Pull yourself together," and I can't.

Pastor Abe: I expect to be interrupted, because that's the role of a priest.

Pastor Dee: Grief is that way, just driving down the street I hear something and I'm right back there, crying, and my mom has been dead over twenty years. You're remembering, crying.

Pastor Abe: For those of you coming from an Asian culture, there has been somewhat of a [negative image] of shamanism. The shaman is the holy person in the community, a person who is connected to the divine. You don't have to say anything—you don't have to make sense. In the West, we have intellectualized everything to death.

Pastor Dee: But sometimes we present ourselves as though we cannot be bothered and so people are put off from calling you. That to me is a shame! We must not give that impression.

Pastor Jeong: One of my colleagues shared an interesting quote with me. He said that the church should not be a social club, but an emergency room. This is a message for our pastoral ministry.

Pastor Betty: The world is really looking for that. Yesterday I was to have lunch downtown. Outside a man was playing a guitar, so I went over and asked him what kind of music he likes. His friend came out, offered me a beer. He had a whole case of them. He asked, "Are you a Christian? I could just tell." He told me he'd had bad experiences [with the church]. The other guy, he is really lost. You're right, Abe, he is just looking for a holy person he can talk to. We prayed together. Then I said, God bless you. Then the other guy said, I want a hug and a blessing, too. I told them, just remember that God loves you, and try to find a fellowship.

Pastor Jeong: That really helped me. I need to redefine the role of the pastor.

Pastor Abe: You have to be available for this job, you have to earn it, and you can't just assume it.

Case 7 (Suicide of a Middle-Aged Man)

This case was presented by Pastor Ben, who serves a United Methodist Church.

About ten years ago, a Stockton man, middle-aged, hanged himself. I heard it had happened, so I took six people with me and we went down to visit. The six of us just listened and listened to the process of sharing. The young man said, "My dad and I had a very good relationship; I was just talking with him yesterday. I am shocked." I wasn't sure I should share this with them, but . . . I told him: There was a man in Laos, one day he left his village and went out into the jungle and hanged himself. About thirty to forty people went hunting for him. It was very hard going in the jungle. My cousin found the body.

Summary of Group Discussion of Case 7

Pastor Jeong: How did the family react to that story?

Pastor Ben: They listened. Perhaps they might think that their father hanging himself just outside the house shows he really cared about them, that they didn't have to go search for his body. That might soften their heart. I don't know. We gathered some money for condolences and presented it to the family at the funeral home. I could see their faces brighten.

Pastor Jeong: Because of your support. And recognizing you as a minister as well?

Pastor Ben: He acknowledged the presence of God in our visit, he brightened. Later, he dropped us a note.

Pastor Jeong: You mentioned the two hours you spent with the family; they must have been in shock. How did you handle that? They must have been very emotional.

Pastor Ben: Yes. I was there for the family and spent hours praying for them, listening to their stories, and took the opportunity to share our sorrow and burden together. I felt that they felt the presence of God.

Pastor Abe: In this culture, how is suicide seen, is it seen as sinful?

Pastor Ben: No, it is generally seen as a choice.

Pastor Jeong: I have encountered pastors who would refuse to do the funeral for a suicide. Three pastors refused one family.

Pastor Dee: I did one funeral for a suicide. Why not? A Roman Catholic church had refused. You should see the grief they had.

Pastor Ben: When you meet with a family regarding a sudden death or a natural death, it's all very similar. I feel you sow a seed that will gradually grow in the family, to feel the presence of God.

Pastor Jeong: At this first meeting with the family, did you mention theology at all?

Pastor Ben: No, I just patiently listened to him say what he needed to say.

Pastor Jeong: Sounds like your story was reassuring to the family.

Pastor Betty: The family was not Christian.

Pastor Ben: Right.

Pastor Betty: But you were being Christ to them. Because you were there, not because you spoke theology.

Pastor Abe: "Preach the gospel at all times, but use words only when necessary."

Pastor Jeong: Sometimes pastors try to put a positive meaning too early, when the death has just happened, trying to soothe the family. Do you think this works?

Pastor Betty: You [the survivors] are not really there, you're on auto-pilot.

Pastor Abe: Never ever.

Pastor Jeong: It could not help you to feel positively about this?

Pastor Abe: No.

Pastor Dee: A youth jumped off the Golden Gate Bridge. All we did when we got to the family home was to sit down and hold their hands. We listened, two hours, just hearing them talk. Then after the adrenaline subsided, I read a passage in the Bible, and then we prayed.

Pastor Ben: Sometimes we need to be a little more active, to discern what needs to be done at that time.

Pastor Betty: As pastors, there's no 1, 2, 3, 4, 5 steps that you do in this situation. No, you just go and pray and see what needs to be done in this situation.

Pastor Ben: The family may need some meaningful scripture reading, maybe they might need something a little more visible.

Pastor Abe: Maybe read Psalm 21, but no explanation, no preaching.

Pastor Dee: I was in shock too. This boy was like my son, too.

Pastor Abe: You were in grief too. Shared in prayer. Shows you're listening. You may mess up, too. It is your presence that will communicate better than any stupid words you may say.

Week 6: Helpful Rituals for Families

Lesson Objective: At the end of the session, the participants will be familiar with ritual resources for creating a space in funeral and memorial services to help those who have lost a loved one to unnatural death (violent death).

Summary of Lesson 6

1. Checklist for preparing rituals and devotions for a family gathering, graveside service, or memorial service (keeping you in check!)

   - Observe what is needed
   - Be present—don't preach; say nothing—let God talk
   - Let those grieving speak first
   - Stay in the present
   - Allow for unexpected times of remembering
   - Verbalize memories
   - Bring memories
   - Facilitate the search for meaning
   - Help the bereaved move beyond grief
   - Help the mourners grieve, then celebrate
   - Know what words *not* to say
   - Choose Scripture
   - Help grievers feel the presence of God
   - Memorialize on the anniversary of the death (one day a year)
   - Send cards as follow-up; acknowledge anniversaries

2. Memorial service ritual "Sharing Memories" (contributed by Rev. Kelly Love, Pastor of Davis United Methodist Church)
   This ritual was used by Pastor Kelly at a service held in remembrance of a gentle young Eagle Scout (given the name

Sam here) who took his own life by gunshot at the age of nineteen.

The instructions to those in attendance at Sam's memorial service for the sharing memories ritual were as follows:

> I want to draw your attention to the blank paper in your bulletin. We are going to share memories of Sam in this service. But your minds and hearts contain more memories than can possibly be shared in one service or even one week. So when your memory is jogged this morning, please use the paper to write down a memory or story— something you remember Sam doing with you or for you, something you remember Sam saying. These memories are our gift to Sam's family, especially his parents. You can keep writing during the reception that follows the service, if you want. You can take your time. There will be baskets in the reception hall that you can leave your papers in, so that Sam's parents can keep them and hold on to those memories.

Following the posting of colors, opening prayer, Scripture readings, hymns, and sermon was the "remembrances." One of Sam's siblings shared the following:

> There are a million memories we could share. I know Mom and Dad want to soak up every one of them. I also know some of you will never stand up in front of a crowd like this to speak, and if that's you, I want there to be time for you to approach Mom and Dad and all the family at the reception and tell them your memories directly. And please, keep writing those memories down on paper to leave with the family, so they have those to hold on to.

At the close of the service, the attendees were invited to continue writing:

"Please continue to write your memories, if you haven't already, and please leave them inside for Sam's family."

Case 8 (Sudden Death of a Choir Member)

This case was presented by Pastor Jess, who serves a United Methodist Church.

I was the Lay Leader and Director of Music for a small Filipino church. . . . Often there would be a memorial on Friday, then the funeral on Saturday, a memorial at forty days, and then a one-year celebration. In some cases, there were nine services, a mixing of religious traditions from the islands and Christianity. There would be a homily, lots of food, hymns, and so on.

We experienced the sudden death of a long-term member, one who was always in the middle of work projects, not up front but always present, a steadfast and beloved worker. He participated in the choir for thirty-some years, and we had a lot of fun together. One Friday morning in choir, as we rehearsed for our upcoming Easter cantata, he didn't feel well. He went home, and that afternoon he died of a sudden aortic aneurism. The difference between an anticipated death from a lingering illness and a sudden traumatic death became really clear in this experience. The following day, on Saturday at choir rehearsal, we could not sing. We had to talk about what had happened to our friend. There was a much greater need for this than if we had been prepared for his death. So, we had a therapy session for all of us. Having done that, we had a memorial on Sunday. There isn't a set ritual for a sudden death, and everybody's equally surprised—the family and the congregation. We decided as a choir to offer a memorial. We loved to sing together as a choir, ages fifteen to seventy-five, a very large group. So at the memorial we did as our friend had often done, got up and sang "He Touched Me" and "Because He Lives."

Throughout the memorial, individuals would sing, others joined in, we cried, told stories, a very spiritual undercurrent just kept stirring which allowed us to spend some of our emotions, becoming a great bridge to calming people down for the memorial and the funeral. A special ritual like this helped us deal with the extreme suddenness of our loss.

Summary of Group Discussion of Case 8

Pastor Abe: I wonder if you put his music on the seat where he always sat in choir. Rituals include the little things that have such power.

Pastor Dee: At one memorial, the seat where he sat, they put flowers there.

Pastor Abe: The memorial book only gets brief signatures when there's a long line waiting. So we furnish cards to fill out name, address, phone, and remembrances, messages to the family. We take a quiet time in the middle of the service for these.

We had a memorial service for a ninety-nine-year-old man (not so sudden a death). He was a wonderful guy but had a very dysfunctional family. All three children said they didn't want a service. So this was a much-anticipated death but also deeply traumatic. We ended up planning a service with other members of the family, and then they all came. The three kids were quite moved and found it incredibly healing. I guess, just a reminder, things around death are not just as they seem. Listen, listen, *listen*! It goes to the top of the list. I don't think it's enough to say, "Be present, don't preach." Before you do anything else, don't do anything, but listen. I'd almost substitute *listen, listen, listen* for the list.

Pastor Jeong: How can we define listening as an element within the ritual?

Pastor Dee: Ritual actually is . . . some people use this as a time to get together but hide their feelings. In some cases, the bereaved put on a cordial show, hide their grief, like everything's okay. I ask myself, Why did we bother? You can never really predict. But I think ritual is still important.

5

Summary and Conclusion

M y project began with the pastoral question, How can pastors better help church members going through traumatic death or losses? Pastors and pastoral caregivers often deal with traumatic death situations such as suicide, but most pastors are not well trained or prepared to minister to suffering families and other survivors who are struggling with spiritual issues and a sense of despair over what seems to them like a meaningless reality.

In this book, I have explored this question from three different perspectives. First, I placed traumatic death in its social and cultural contexts. I examined the incidence of violence in the United States. In particular, I explored some of the social factors that might cause suicide. This approach opened up the topic and is a reminder that suicide is not purely an individual issue but offers a challenge to society. If the church is a community, i.e., a social system, then suicide calls the church to engage in a social mission with those who are on the edge of the community's care and attention.

Second, I viewed traumatic death through a psychological lens. From a psychological perspective, trauma is a crisis. Traumatic death traumatizes the survivor and disrupts his or her life. Since traumatic death occurs suddenly and without warning, it is often more difficult to grieve this type of death than other deaths. Those who have lost their loved one from a traumatic death typically struggle with unique and intense emotional, psychological, and spiritual (theological) challenges. In the case of a traumatic death, the bereaved and survivors often express a strong sense of guilt.

Second, in our society there is still a stigma associated with suicide. The survivors are the ones who have to suffer the shame after a family member takes his or her own life, and their sense of shame can be influenced by the reactions of others. Another unique feature of sudden death is the sense of *helplessness* that it elicits in the survivor. Often, this helplessness is linked with an incredible sense of rage, and it is not unusual for the survivor to want to vent his or her anger at someone. Lastly, traumatic grief is often associated with feelings that life is empty or meaningless without the person who died. Finding meaning in the death of a loved one can be an extremely traumatic and difficult task for the victim's survivors. For the work of healing and strengthening resilience, I have found Edward K. Rynearson's method of "restorative retelling" to be a very helpful tool for supporting the survivors of traumatic death. In traumatic grief, storying is an important part of the healing process because it helps the survivors make meaning of what seems like a meaningless event.

Third, I viewed the challenge of trauma from two theological perspectives and attempted to help pastors and spiritual caregivers find theological meaning in traumatic death. Traumatic death, however, is a meaningless event. A traumatic death is also more likely to provoke the spiritually despairing question in survivors, "Why did God allow this horror to happen to us?" Survivors suffer from despair, especially in relation to the question of why God was powerless in the situation. "Why is God so helpless and voiceless in this tragic death?" I proposed the metaphor of God as a "fellow sufferer" as a better image for the bereaved and those traumatized by a tragic death. I explored the contributions of two contemporary theologians regarding the theodicy issue: Gregory Anderson Love and Andrew Sung Park. First, Love understands God as a compassionate God who feels our suffering and stays with us in the midst of our pain. That is what Emmanuel God ('God is with us') means in our life. The cross of Jesus in Christian spirituality portrays a merciful and forgiving God who hears our cries and watches over our pain in a desperate and suffering reality, and God in a human form came to us and was willing to die on the cross to save us. Second, Park's theological lens helps pastors and spiritual caregivers to expand their understanding of sin to consider the suffering of the victims of sin. Park reminds us of the basic pastoral care principle that no power in the universe can make God vulnerable, but a victim's suffering breaks the heart of God. We may look to a new image of a vulnerable God in the cross.

Love and Park both emphasized the compassion of God, but they seem to have a different understanding of God's nature. Love follows St. Anselm's understanding of God as an impassible and unchangeable God. God won't be angry at us, nor does God change God's plan because of our situation. Park seems to understand that a victim's suffering may appeal to and influence the heart of God. In other words, whereas Love focuses on God's own substance (personality) as a "compassionate God" who is willing to initiate and restore our broken relationships, Park emphasizes that the victim's reality of suffering may play a significant role in changing God's plan and direction because God is ardent, merciful, and compassionate to the victim. For those who face a spiritual crisis due to a traumatic death, I believe that pastors who are trained to deal with ultimate questions of meaning and value can help the bereaved rediscover that living in relationship with a loving and faithful God provides meaning in the midst of tragedy.

I also describe in this book a six-week project on grief caused by traumatic death. Seven United Methodist pastors agreed to participate in the project. Every participant expressed that at first they did not really understand that traumatic death has unique consequences for the grief of survivors. The word *violence* was a key word for the participants that helped them understand the dynamics of traumatic death. As the sessions went on, the participants began to be able to clearly identify traumatic death as violent death. There were several 'a-ha moments' and new learnings as a result of the sessions.

- First, responding to a traumatic death is a type of crisis care because it involves traumatic loss and causes a psychological and spiritual crisis.

- Second, *listening* is the most powerful spiritual intervention in caring for souls, but sometimes pastors forget this basic approach even in dealing with traumatic death and loss.

- Lastly, spiritual care and the preparation of a memorial or funeral service ought to be designed to care for those who are hurting and to share stories about the deceased.

The essence of traumatic death is violence. Family members who have lost a loved one struggle with their feelings of victimization. This type of pastoral care requires spiritual leaders not simply to understand the difference between regular death and traumatic death but also to care for the family in crisis and offer meaningful rituals and services to help people find hidden meaning in a meaningless event. As spiritual leaders, pastors are called to guide their congregants, journeying with them as a companion, not as their problem solver. I hope that this project will enhance spiritual leaders' awareness of this topic and help them prepare meaningful rituals that a family who has lost their loved one can use to find hope, even in what feels like a hopeless and meaningless situation.

Psychological theories and theological insights from Love and Park offer the important perspective of traumatic death as a psychological and spiritual crisis. The larger reality of traumatic death is based on the social and systemic contexts and the complicated grief process is based on the psychological context of the bereaved. Psychological theories help differentiate the traumatic death bereavement task from grief work related to ordinary death and also identify the role of the church as a community responsible for its members. The theological material helps spiritual leaders envision a relevant God who will comfort and care for mourners and those who are wounded spiritually and psychologically.

So, I return to the question that I began with: "How can pastors better help church members going through traumatic death or loss?" In light of my research and the project I conducted, what advice or guidance would I now give pastors and other spiritual leaders on this subject? Let me note six lessons.

Know that your presence (not your words) is one of the most critical tools you have to comfort those in shock from a traumatic loss. God as fellow sufferer is a powerful and challenging pastoral care model for modern pastors. God is not hesitant or reluctant to be there with us when we desperately ask for God's gracious presence. Jesus was willing to "be there" on the cross for us. Our God as companion, friend, and fellow sojourner with each human being always reminds us to keep the first basic and essential pastoral care principle, the power of presence, in our mind and heart and at the center of our pastoral ministry. God is not up on a throne but is here and wants to be with us always. We should remember that our pastoral presence is one of the most critical and effective ministry tools we have, especially for those who are suffering and going through a difficult time due to a traumatic loss and grief.

Be prepared to listen to the retelling and continuing discussions close family members need to do to help them with the "why" question. Train yourself to be a good companion, and be especially mindful and careful in the words and phrases you use. Some of the standard phrases used to comfort those dealing with death and dying do not apply to traumatic loss, where guilt and shame often exist. For example, do not say these words to comfort the survivors of traumatic loss:

"I know how you feel."

"I understand."

"It was God's will."

"He/she is better off/in a better place/happier now."

"Out of tragedies good things happen."

"You'll get over it."

"Time heals all wounds."

"You should get on with your life."

"She/he led a good and full life before she/he died."

"Your loved one didn't suffer when he/she died."[1]

---

1. Schipani, "Pastoral Care in Crisis Situations," class lecture, summer

Grow in your understanding of God. Be open to seeing God not as an emperor or king but as a fellow sufferer, as one who can embrace the horrible pain survivors of traumatic loss experience. Revisit your own theological and pastoral understanding of God as you face traumatic deaths and losses and offer God's comfort and care to those who struggle with meaningless realities. What is a good image of God that does not conflict with the image of the almighty God?

Perform special rituals. Sometimes the standard rituals do not apply to people going through a traumatic death. The pastors who participated in the project taught me that sometimes we must be creative; we must create our own rituals or enhance the standard memorial service in ways that better meet the needs of the family. Rituals must facilitate silent communication with the survivors and help to remove the isolation that often accompanies a traumatic loss.

Reach out to other pastors who have supported survivors of traumatic loss within their congregation and/or community. Pastors do not need to face this spiritual crisis alone. Our colleagues in ministry often have wisdom born of years of experience in such matters. The more we gather together to share the traumatic loss, the more we will help to remove the social stigma that is often associated with traumatic loss, in particular with suicide.

Sign up for a continuing education course that focuses on pastoral care to support survivors of traumatic loss or organize your own group of pastors and other spiritual leaders. Generally speaking, the incidence of violent death is growing, and although caring for the bereaved has been at the heart of pastoral ministry, few pastors are trained to counsel people experiencing sudden death and complicated grief. The survivors of a traumatic death struggle with the death and with finding hope and God's mercy and grace in the middle of the chaos, questions, and confusion. Unfortunately, most pastors are not well trained in how to provide appropriate pastoral care and spiritual presence. I believe that the importance of pastoral care in sudden death is not only an issue of improving a

2014.

pastor's competency but also an important concern for the life and growth of the church in general. If pastors do not know how to be fully present with those who are in anger and despair, those who are struggling with the lack of a sense of the presence of God, this deficit may result in people losing their faith.

My work on my dissertation/project and on this book has helped me tremendously in learning how to prepare for dealing with traumatic death and losses in my parish ministry as a spiritual leader. The most valuable idea that I have learned and gained from all of my work on my dissertation is the importance of compassion. I was able to re-open my spiritual eyes to see God as a compassionate God who understands our pain and hears our cries and to view Jesus as the Son of God who was willing to take up the cross. Jesus promised us that God will always be with us as Emmanuel God. While I was exploring the issues related to traumatic death grief work, I realized that Jesus truly wanted to share the compassion of God with his disciples and followers. If I have the opportunity to lead this project again in the future, I will explore images of God in the Bible, especially acts that reflect God's compassion, and I will present a new image of God as a compassionate God. And, I am interested in whether the image of a compassionate God leads to any conflict or contradiction with the almighty and powerful God in the Bible.

Focusing on compassion is a powerful way to understand God in the Christian tradition. The Christian belief that God who is beyond our understanding encounters us in the form of humanity, suffering our pain and even suffering death on the cross, clearly represents God's radically compassionate nature. This is the essence of the theological meaning of God's incarnation, death, and resurrection as the radical promise of God's presence with us as Emmanuel God. Compassion with the promise of divine presence is the core of the Judeo-Christian faith tradition throughout the entire biblical world, both in the Old Testament and the New Testament. The compassionate God will never leave us to suffer alone but will always be with us in our desperate need and trouble. In other words, one form of compassion as enacted by pastors is being present in a caring way with the survivors of traumatic loss. Truly, this is what I discovered about compassion through the process of writing this book—that the power of presence is the genuine way God works in the world.

Bibliography

American Association of Suicidology. "U.S.A. Suicide: 2013 Official Final Data." http://www.suicidology.org/Portals/14/docs/Resources/FactSheets/2013datapgsv3.pdf.

American Foundation for Suicide Prevention, "Facts and Figures." https://www.afsp.org/understanding-suicide/facts-and-figures.

American Psychiatric Association. *Diagnostic and Statistical Manual of Mental Disorders.* 5th ed. Washington, DC: American Psychiatric Association, 2013.

Anderson, Herbert. "Common Grief, Complex Grieving." *Pastoral Psychology* 59 (2010) 127–36.

Andreasen, Nancy C. "Post-traumatic Stress Disorder." In *Comprehensive Textbook of Psychiatry,* 4th ed., edited by Harold I. Kaplan and Benjamin J. Sadock (pp. 918–24). Baltimore: Lippincott Williams & Wilkins, 1985.

Augsburger, David W. *Pastoral Counseling across Cultures.* 1st ed. Philadelphia: Westminster, 1986.

Becvar, Dorothy S. *In the Presence of Grief: Helping Family Members Resolve Death, Dying, and Bereavement Issues.* New York: Guilford, 2001.

Beder, Joan. *Voices of Bereavement: A Casebook for Grief Counselors.* Series in Death, Dying, and Bereavement. New York: Brunner-Routledge, 2004.

Billman, Kathleen D., and Daniel L. Migliore. *Rachel's Cry: Prayer of Lament and Rebirth of Hope.* Eugene, OR: Wipf and Stock Publishers, 2007.

Bolton, Iris. *My Son . . . My Son . . . : A Guide to Healing After Death, Loss and Suicide.* Atlanta: Bolton, 1983.

Boss, Pauline. *Loss, Trauma, and Resilience: Therapeutic Work with Ambiguous Loss.* New York: W. W. Norton, 2006.

Bowlby, John. *Attachment and Loss: Loss, Sadness and Depression.* Vol. 3. New York: Basic Books, 1973.

———. *Separation: Anxiety and Anger. Attachment and Loss.* Vol. 2. New York: Basic Books, 1973.

Brock, Rita Nakashima, and Gabriella Lentini. *Soul Repair: Recovering from Moral Injury after War.* Boston: Beacon, 2012.

Bueckert, Leah Dawn, and Daniel S. Schipani, eds. *Spiritual Caregiving in the Hospital: Windows to Chaplaincy Ministry.* Rev. ed. Kitchener, ON, Canada: Pandora, 2011.

Cain, Albert C. *Survivors of Suicide.* Springfield, IL: Charles C. Thomas, 1972.

Carder, Kenneth L. "Why Follow a Crucified Christ?" *Christian Century,* Aug. 27–Sept. 3, 1997, p. 753.

Carson D. A. *How Long, O Lord? Reflections on Suffering and Evil.* Grand Rapids, MI: Baker Academic, 2006.

Centers for Disease Control and Prevention. "About SUID and SIDS." http://www.cdc.gov/sids/aboutsuidandsids.htm.

———. Suicide: Facts at a Glance 2015." http://www.cdc.gov/violenceprevention/pdf/suicide-datasheet-a.pdf.

———. "Suicides Due to Alcohol and/or Drug Overdose: A Data Brief from the National Violent Death Reporting System." http://www.cdc.gov/violenceprevention/nvdrs/nvdrs_data_brief.html.

Cisney, Jennifer S., and Kevin L. Ellers. *The First 48 Hours: Spiritual Caregivers as First Responders.* Nashville: Abingdon, 2008.

Clemons, James T. *What Does the Bible Say about Suicide?* Minneapolis: Fortress, 1990.

Clinebell, Howard. *Basic Types of Pastoral Care and Counseling: Resources for the Ministry of Healing and Growth.* Rev. ed. Nashville: Abingdon, 1984.

Cobain, Beverly, and Jean Larch. *Dying to Be Free: A Healing Guide for Families after a Suicide.* Center City, MN: Hazelden Foundation, 2006.

Cole, Allan Hugh, Jr. *Good Mourning: Getting through Your Grief.* Louisville, KY: Westminster, 2008.

Colgrove, Melba, Harold H. Bloomfield, and Peter McWilliams. *How to Survive the Loss of a Love.* New York: Leo, 1976.

Deits, Bob, *Life after Loss: Practical Guide to Renewing Your Life after Experiencing Major Loss.* Cambridge, MA: Da Capo, 2004.

Doka, Kenneth J., and Anita L. Bradshaw. *Clergy to Clergy: Helping You Minister to Those Confronting Illness, Death and Grief* (sound recording). Washington DC: Hospital Foundation of America. 1994.

———. *Disenfranchised Grief: New Directions, Challenges, and Strategies for Practice.* Champaign, IL: Research, 2002.

Doyle, Polly. *Grief Counseling and Sudden Death: A Manual and Guide.* Springfield, IL: Charles C. Thomas, 1980.

Duivendyk, Tim. *The Unwanted Gift of Grief: A Ministry Approach.* London: Routledge, 2006.

Durkheim, Émile. *The Rules of Sociological Method and Selected Texts on Sociology and Its Method.* Translated by W. D. Halls. New York: Free, 1982.

Dyer, Kirsti A. "Dealing with Sudden, Accidental or Traumatic Death." Journey of Hearts. http://www.journeyofhearts.org/grief/accident2.html.

Floyd, Scott. *Crisis Counseling: A Guide to Pastors and Professionals.* Grand Rapids, MI: Kregel Publications, 2008.

Fowler, Gene. *Caring through the Funeral: A Pastor's Guide.* St. Louis, MO: Chalice, 2004.

Friedman, Maurice. "Martin Buber's 'Narrow Ridge.'" In *Martin Buber and the Human Sciences,* edited by Maurice Friedman, 3–25. Albany, NY: SUNY Press, 1996.

Gallagher, Janette. "The Unique, Complicated Grief of Suicide." Class handout in Daniel S. Schipani's class "Pastoral Care in Crisis Situations: Loss, Grief and Trauma in Theological and Psychological Perspective," May 29, 2014, San Francisco Theological Seminary, San Anselmo, California.

Gilbert, Kathleen R. "Traumatic Loss and the Family." http://www.familyresource.com/relationships/grief-and-loss/traumatic-loss-and-the-family.

———. "'We've Had the Same Loss, Why Don't We Have the Same Grief?'" Family Meanings and Family Grief." GriefNet Library: Families and Grief. http://griefnet.org/library/families.html.

Glick, Ira Oscar, Robert S. Weiss, and Colin Murray Parkes. *The First Year of Bereavement.* New York: John Wiley & Sons, 1974.

Goldston, David B., Sherry Davis Molock, Leslie B. Whitbeck, Jessica L. Murakami, Luis H. Zayas, and Gordon C. Nagayama Hall. "Cultural Considerations in Adolescent Suicide Prevention and Psychosocial Treatment." *American Psychologist* 63, no. 1 (January 2008) 14–31.

Grief Speaks. "Cultures and Grief." http://www.griefspeaks.com/id90.html.

———. "Understanding Cultural Issues in Death." Grief Speaks. http://www.griefspeaks.com/id90.html.

Harvard Injury Control Research Center. "Firearms Research: Suicide." http://www.hsph.harvard.edu/hicrc/firearms-research/gun-ownership-and-use/.

Harvey, John H., ed. *Perspectives on Loss: A Sourcebook.* Series in Death, Dying, and Bereavement. Abingdon, UK: Routledge, 1998.

Hauerwas, Stanley. *God, Medicine, and Suffering.* Grand Rapids, MI: Wm. B. Eerdmans Publishing, 1994.

Herman, Judith, *Trauma and Recovery.* New York: Basic Books, 1997.

Hewett, John H. *After Suicide.* Louisville, KY: Westminster John Knox, 1980.

Howarth, Glennys. *Death and Dying: A Sociological Introduction.* Cambridge, UK: Polity, 2007.

Hsu, Albert Y., *Grieving Suicide: A Loved One's Search for Comfort, Answers and Hope.* Downers Grove, IL: InterVarsity, 2002.

Humphrey, Geraldine M., & David G. Zimpfer. *Counselling for Grief and Bereavement.* 2nd ed. Counselling in Practice. Los Angeles: Sage Publications, 2008.

James, John W., and Frank Cherry. *The Grief Recovery Handbook: A Step-by-Step Program for Moving beyond Loss.* New York: HarperPerennial, 1988.

James, John W., and Russell Friedman. *The Grief Recovery Handbook: The Action Program for Moving beyond Death, Divorce, and Other Losses.* New York: HarperCollins Publishers, 1998.

Jones, Serene. *Trauma and Grace: Theology in a Ruptured World.* Louisville, KY: Westminster John Knox, 2009.

Jordan, John R. "Is Suicide Bereavement Different? A Reassessment of the Literature." *Suicide and Life-Threatening Behavior* 31, no. 1 (Spring 2011) 91–102.

Kavanaugh, Robert E. *Facing Death.* Baltimore, MD: Penguin Books, 1974.

Kelley, Melissa. *Grief: Contemporary Theory and the Practice of Ministry.* Minneapolis, MN: Fortress, 2010.

Koenig, Harold G. *In the Wake of Disaster: Religious Responses to Terrorism and Catastrophe.* West Conshohocken, PA: Templeton Foundation, 2006.

Kübler-Ross, Elisabeth, and David Kessler. *On Grief and Grieving: Finding the Meaning of Grief through the Five Stages of Loss.* New York: Scribner, 2005.

Laato, Antti, and de Moore, Johannes C. *Theodicy in the World of the Bible.* Leiden, The Netherlands: Brill Academic, 2003.

Lartey, Emmanuel Yartekwei. *In Living Color: An Intercultural Approach to Pastoral Care and Counseling.* 2nd ed. London: Jessica Kingsley Publishers, 2003.

Lehman, Darrin R., John H. Ellard, and Camille B. Wortman. "Social Support for the Bereaved: Recipients' and Providers' Perspectives on What Is Helpful." *Journal of Consulting and Clinical Psychology* 54, no. 4 (August 1986) 438–46.

Lehmann, Linda, Shane R. Jimerson, and Ann Gaasch. *Grief Support Group Curriculum: Facilitator's Handbook.* Philadelphia: Brunner-Routledge, 2001.

Lester, Andrew D. *Hope in Pastoral Care and Counseling.* Louisville, KY: Westminster John Knox, 1995.

Lewis, C. S. *A Grief Observed.* London: Faber and Faber, 1961.

Lindemann, Erich. "Symptomatology and Management of Acute Grief." *American Journal of Psychiatry* 101 (1944) 141–48.

Love, Gregory Anderson, *Love, Violence, and the Cross: How the Nonviolent God Saves Us through the Cross of Christ.* Eugene, OR: Cascade Publications, 2010.

Margolis, Otto S., ed. *Acute Grief: Counseling the Bereaved.* Foundations of Thanatology Series. New York: Columbia University Press, 1981.

Martin, Sherry Hendricks. *Beginning Again: Tools for the Journey through Grief.* Edmond, OK: Greystone, 2006.

McCall, Junietta Baker, and Harold G. Koenig. *Bereavement Counseling: Pastoral Care for Complicated Grieving.* New York: Routledge, 2004.

Miller, Matthew, Deborah Azrael, and David Hemenway. "Household Firearm Ownership Levels and Suicide across U.S. Regions and States, 1988–1997." *Epidemiology* 13 (2002) 517–24.

Miller, Matthew, Steven Lippmann, Deborah Azrael, and David Hemenway. "Household Firearm Ownership and Rates of Suicide across U.S. States." *Journal of Trauma* 62 (2007) 1029–35.

Mitchell, Kenneth R., and Anderson, Herbert. *All Our Losses, All Our Griefs: Resources for Pastoral Care.* Louisville, KY: Westminster John Knox, 1983.

Moncher, Frank J., Rosella L. Allison, and Arthur A. Bennett. *Coping with a Suicide: Catholic Teaching and Pastoral Response.* New Haven, CT: Knights of Columbus Supreme Council, 2008.

Mottram, Kenneth P. *Caring for Those in Crisis: Facing Ethical Dilemmas with Patients and Families.* Grand Rapids, MI: Brazos, 2007.

Murphy, Shirley A., L. Clark Johnson, and Janet Lohan. "Finding Meaning in a Child's Violent Death: A Five-Year Prospective Analysis of Parents' Personal Narratives and Empirical Data." *Death Studies* 27, no. 5 (2003) 381–404.

Oates, Wayne Edward. *Grief, Transition, and Loss: A Pastor's Practical Guide.* Creative Pastoral Care and Counseling Series. Minneapolis: Augsburg Fortress, 1997.

Oswald, Roy. *Transforming Rituals: Daily Practices for Changing Lives.* Washington, DC: Alban Institute, 1999.

Park, Andrew Sung. *From Hurt to Healing: Theology of the Wounded.* Nashville: Abingdon, 2004.

————. *The Wounded Heart of God: The Asian Concept of Han and the Christian Doctrine of Sin.* Nashville: Abingdon, 1993.

Parkes, Colin Murray. *Love and Loss: The Roots of Grief and Its Complications.* London: Routledge, 2006.

Ramshaw, Elaine. *Ritual and Pastoral Care.* Theology and Pastoral Care Series. Philadelphia: Fortress, 1987.

Rando, Therese A. *Grief, Dying, and Death: Clinical Interventions for Caregivers.* Champaign, IL: Research, 1984.

————. *Loss and Anticipatory Grief.* New York: Lexington Books, 1986.

————. *Treatment of Complicated Mourning.* Champaign, IL: Research, 1993.

Roman Catholic Church. Cathechism of the Catholic Church, Part Three: Life in Christ. http://www.vatican.va/archive/ccc_css/archive/catechism/p3s2c2a5.htm.

Rupp, Joyce. *Praying Our Goodbyes: A Spiritual Companion through Life's Losses and Sorrows.* Notre Dame, IN: Ave Maria, 2009.

Rynearson, Edward K. "Accommodation to Unnatural Death." Violent Death Bereavement Society, 2006. http://www.vdbs.org/docs/Accommodation%20to%20Unnatural%20Death%20-%20Revised%207-06-1.pdf.

————. *Retelling Violent Death.* New York: Brunner-Routledge, 2001.

————. *Violent Death: Resilience and Intervention beyond the Crisis.* New York: Routledge, 2006.

Schipani, Daniel S. "Pastoral Care in Crisis Situations: Loss, Grief and Trauma in Theological and Psychological Perspective." Class lectures, summer 2014, San Francisco Theological Seminary, San Anselmo, CA.

Seaver, Pat. *Preparing Liturgies for Victims of Suicide*. Blackrock, Ireland: Columbia, 2006.

Sieckert, Kris. "Cultural Perspectives on Trauma and Crisis Response." http:// crisisresourceguide.weebly.com/uploads/2/0/3/8/20381783/cultural_ perspectives_on_trauma_and_critical_response.pdf. [condensed version of chapter 7 of the National Organization for Victim Assistance (NOVA) *Community Response Team Training Manual*, 2nd ed. Washington, DC: NOVA, 1998]

Stone, Howard W. *Crisis Counseling*. 3rd ed. Creative Pastoral Care and Counseling Series. Minneapolis: Fortress, 2009.

———. *Suicide and Grief*. Philadelphia: Fortress, 1972.

———. *Theological Context for Pastoral Caregiving: Word in Deed*. Binghamton, NY: Haworth, 1996.

Stroebe, Margaret S., Wolfgang Stroebe, and Robert O. Hansson. *Handbook of Bereavement: Theory, Research, and Intervention*. Cambridge, UK: Cambridge University Press, 1993.

Sullender, R. Scott. *Grief and Growth: Pastoral Resources for Emotional and Spiritual Growth*. Mahwah, NJ: Paulist, 1985.

———. "Loss, Grief and Trauma." Class lecture, Feb. 21, 2013, San Francisco Theological Seminary, San Anselmo, California.

———. *Losses in Later Life: A New Way of Walking with God*. New York: Haworth, 1999.

Townsend, Lauren L. *Suicide: Pastoral Responses*. Nashville: Abingdon, 2006.

Walsh, Froma. *Strengthening Family Resilience*. New York: Guilford, 1998.

Ware, Patti. *Bereavement Ministry Manual with Study Guide: A Scriptural Approach to Comforting Those in Mourning*. Createspace Independent Publishing Platform, 2008.

Weaver, Andrew J., Laura T. Flannelly, and John D. Preston. *Counseling Survivors of Traumatic Events: A Handbook for Pastors and Other Helping Professionals*. Nashville: Abingdon, 2003.

Westberg, Granger E. *Good Grief: A Constructive Approach to the Problem of Loss*. Philadelphia: Fortress, 1984.

Wikipedia, "Crime in the United States," accessed Nov. 9, 2015, https:// en.wikipedia.org/wiki/Crime_in_the_United_States.

Wikipedia, "Suicide," accessed November 19, 2015, http://en.wikipedia.org/ wiki/Suicide#cite_note-GDB2013-4.

Wikipedia, "United States Military Veteran Suicide," accessed Nov. 9, 2015, http://en.wikipedia.org/wiki/United_States_military_veteran_suicide_ epidemic.

Williams, Margo. *And Then There Was One: Our Journey from Death to Rebirth*. Eau Claire, MI: Pooka, 1996.

Wolfelt, Alan D. *Creating Meaningful Funeral Ceremonies: A Guide for Caregivers*. Fort Collins, CO: Companion, 1994.

———. *The Wilderness of Suicide Grief: Finding Your Way*. Fort Collins, CO: Companion, 2010.

Wolterstorff, Nicholas. *Lament for a Son*. Grand Rapids, MI: Wm. B. Eerdmans, 1987.

Worden, J. William. *Grief Counseling and Grief Therapy: A Handbook for the Mental Health Professional*. 4th ed. New York: Springer Publishing, 2009.

World Health Organization. *Preventing Suicide: A Global Imperative*. Geneva, Switzerland: World Health Organization, 2014. http://apps.who.int/iris/bitstream/10665/131056/1/9789241564779_eng.pdf.

————. "Suicide Data," accessed November 19, 2015, http://www.who.int/mental_health/prevention/suicide/suicideprevent/en/.

Wright, H. Norman. *The New Guide to Crisis and Trauma Counseling*. Ventura, CA: Regal Books, 2003.

————. *Recovering from Losses in Life*. Grand Rapids, MI: Fleming H. Revell, 2006.

York, Sarah. *Remembering Well: Rituals for Celebrating Life and Mourning Death*. San Francisco: Jossey-Bass, 2000.

Young, Harriet. *Bereavement Ministry: A Leader's Resource Manual*. Mystic, CT: Twenty-Third Publications, 1997.

Young, Marlene. *Community Response Team Training Manual* (2nd ed.). Washington, DC: NOVA, 1998.

Zucker, Robert. "The Challenge of Restorative Retelling Following a Violent Death: A Conversation with Edward Rynears." Robert Zucker. Accessed Dec. 29, 2015. http://robertzucker.com/articles/38-the-challenge-of-restorative-retelling-following-a-violent-death-a-conversation-with-edward-rynears.html.